WHEN MOMMY GROWS UP

A GUIDE TO PARENTING YOURSELF TO A MORE
FULFILLING CAREER

BECCA CARNAHAN

Rise

An Imprint of Clear Fork Publishing

When Mommy Grows Up

Summary: *When Mommy Grows Up: A Guide to Parenting Yourself to a More Fulfilling Career* is a relatable and funny career development book for moms that reframes lessons we teach our children as career advice. It invites moms to learn more about themselves, define what success looks like to them, achieve their goals, and find the humor along the way.

Clear Fork Publishing

P.O. Box 870 102 S. Swenson Stamford, Texas 79553 (915)209-0003

www.clearforkpublishing.com

Printed in the United States of America

Softcover ISBN - 978-1-950169-51-1

Ebook ISBN - 978-1-950169-52-8

LCN - 2021935832

To Merm and Pop.
For teaching me how to laugh at myself, believe in myself, and be
myself every step of the way.

CONTENTS

PROLOGUE

*I*n the summer of 2016, I had a life-changing conversation with a stranger at the Department of Motor Vehicles. The DMV isn't exactly known as a place to build lasting friendships. It's a place you go out of necessity and a place you complain about before, during, and after your visit. But that day, I left the DMV with a renewed license and a renewed outlook on life, and without that stranger, I'm quite certain this book would not exist.

At the time, I was days away from turning 31 years old, weeks removed from having my second baby in two years, and probably looked like I could have used a shower. Or seven showers. Kenzie, my new DMV friend, was taller than me by about three inches, which was impressive in itself considering my WNBA-level stature. She was also rocking some very cool tattoos and the confidence of a person who knew who she was and who she wanted to become. Most importantly, Kenzie was very friendly, my baby daughter was sleeping, and there was nowhere to go, so we settled into a comfortable conversation while waiting for our numbers to be called.

As we waited, Kenzie and I covered the weather, Boston traffic, and our feelings about waiting in long lines. Then somehow, the conversation took a sharp left, and we found ourselves in an in-depth discussion about heartbreaks, family dynamics, and broken dreams. Things got real, and if memory serves, I unsuccessfully tried to dry my tears with a baby wipe. We ventured back into lighter conversational territory after a bit, which made sense since we had met 30 minutes ago at the DMV. Or at least Kenzie considered what was next to be lighter conversational territory. I was about to have my world rocked.

I asked Kenzie what she did for a living, and she returned the question. We spoke about our jobs – her work driving delivery trucks for a large furniture distributor and my work at Harvard Business School in career services. Then Kenzie told me about her motorcycle, the old cars she was fixing up, and one very amusing story about underestimating the difficulty involved in hiking a mountain with a backpack full of beer.

I knew what was coming next. Kenzie was going to ask me about my hobbies.

She did, to which I replied, "Keeping my two small children alive."

Kenzie and I laughed at my standard-issue mom joke, but since we had forged a deep bond, and according to the sign at the DMV, we still had 4,586 numbers to go before we were called, she pushed me on the point.

"But what else? Like before you had kids. What makes you who you are?"

I panicked, then quickly turned into a walking cliché and said, "I like watching sports and spending time with my family and friends." In my dramatic retelling of this story,

Kenzie always yawns. But in reality, she didn't; she was lovely.

The conversation stuck with me for several reasons. Kenzie was at the DMV changing the sex on her license so her ID would represent the strong, proud woman she was today. I'll never forget her story and all she had to fight through to be herself. She was also one of the most interesting people I had ever met, filled to the brim with passions, hopes, and dreams. I walked away, feeling like I owed her more. Like I owed myself, my kids, and the world more.

Here I sat, a suburban mom and wife with a couple of university degrees, a couple of kids, a growing career, and a long list of privileges I had been born into yet my list of interesting personal factoids stopped at watching Monday Night Football? Of course, keeping my kids alive (and clothed, clean, educated, etc.) was critical and meaningful work and a role I had pined over for years. I also enjoyed the work I was doing in the higher education industry and had put a ton of effort into building my career. Yet Kenzie stirred up this feeling that I hadn't explored something else inside me or let myself even consider exploring. Meanwhile, Kenzie had faced discrimination, loss, and financial hardship, and she was out there taking the bull by the horns, not holding anything back. Where was my bull? Sure, I was working hard going about the everyday tasks of my life, but I wasn't grabbing anyone's horns.

Six months later, after finally showering and getting some much-needed sleep, I replayed the conversation back in my mind. It was then I realized I wanted to tell Kenzie what I really liked doing was writing funny status updates on Facebook. Quipping and storytelling were a part of my DNA, but I had never considered expanding on that beyond a few hastily scrolled comments about the funny things my kids did that day or my thoughts and feelings about mashed potatoes. Perhaps writing could be my own thing in this crazy world of new motherhood and help me figure out what makes me who I am or who I was becoming. Maybe it could be my small way of helping someone else by making them feel less alone or simply making them laugh. That's how my conversation with Kenzie at the DMV inspired the very first post on my blog, "With Love, Becca," a funny and heartfelt love letter to moms managing motherhood, managing careers, and managing to laugh through it all.

———

Now that I had my blog, I could go back and find Kenzie at the DMV and tell her I write funny articles about toddler bedtime routines, working mom hacks, and 90s nostalgia in my free time. That felt good, and writing felt like this exciting extension of myself. It put me in a feeling of flow I hadn't experienced in a long time. But finding a hobby I loved led to another itch. An itch that was telling me, "Okay, Becca, good work, but you don't think this personal development stuff is over, right? We're just getting started, sweetheart."

Despite the slightly condescending tone of my subconscious, I knew without a doubt, this was correct. Motherhood and writing had both changed me at a core level, so it was time to rethink how I evaluated my life and career success. Perhaps success didn't mean climbing a ladder of promotions; it meant doing work I loved as often as possible so that time away from my kids counted. Maybe success was somehow stepping off the hamster wheel of a long commute, eight hours of work, and screeching into daycare on two wheels so that life didn't feel like such a whirlwind.

Defining success for yourself and then going for it was precisely what I had been talking to the students at Harvard about for years. However, it took a trip to the DMV and writing many blog posts that referenced mid-90s teen heart-throbs to make me realize I was not fully internalizing these lessons myself.

I had gotten too comfortable being kind of uncomfortable, which is a weird phrase, but I think you know what I mean. I was leaning into my career's safety and stability without pausing to consider if I was tackling the right kind of challenges and being the best version of myself, or if I was stuffing myself into boxes.

Creative Becca goes here.

Career Coaching Becca goes there.

Manager Becca goes here.

Mom Becca goes there.

Then all of those Becca boxes get crowded into a Toyota Corolla, listening to top country music hits three hours a day.

It was scary to think about making a change and getting out of my boxes and out of my car, but people change. Our interests change, our skills change, the skills we want to use change. Parenthood changes you.

I wasn't alone on this island either.

Far from it. As I chatted with other moms of young kids at the playground and they found out I worked in career development and wrote about working mom life, our conversations quickly went from Paw Patrol Band-Aids to discussing career plans.

They wondered aloud, "What's next for me? Is the path I carved out for myself ten years ago still the right fit? Can I incorporate more flexibility into my work life to do all the things I want to do with my family? And can I even pause long enough from ensuring my kids don't scale the park fence to think about all that, let alone get there?"

These mothers were my people, and I wanted to use all of my career development experience to help them get past their mental blocks of "Well, guess I'll just be moderately happy and stressed and do this until I retire?" and find something that worked better. I clearly remember sitting across from a friend at a park picnic table in fall 2017, promising I would figure this all out for myself and then help others walk their paths.

Since it was a pinky swear type promise, I kept it, which leads us to today and this book. Four years removed from my DMV chat with Kenzie and three years removed from the picnic table promise, I've figured out what I wanted to be when I grew up next and made those significant changes that seemed so scary a few years ago.

The first change was turning my blog into a business I love. By breaking down the walls of my Becca boxes, I built a website that lets me be creative, professional, and a funny mom while reaching hundreds of thousands of people and bringing in an income for my family. Then I turned to my 9-5 career services work and learned how to turn the job I had into a job I loved again. I started offering to take on writing projects to flex my creative muscles, and at the same time, I grabbed every opportunity to learn and grow as a career coach. From there, I opened up my career coaching practice to do even more coaching and take those playground career conversations with other moms to the next level. I became a side hustling pro and reignited the passion I needed to make being a working mom work for me and not against me.

As for that pesky three-hour commute? After twelve years at Harvard Business School, I packed up my office and waved goodbye to both the job title I had earned and the building that had been my professional home for most of my life. Now I work from home and for myself. I'm rocking leggings most days and a dash of lipstick some days, and I'm in control of the writing projects I take on, the coaching clients I work with, and how much time I get to spend with my family.

There was a long lead up to that day and a ton of work, but it was worth it because I took the time to figure out what I wanted and then put in the blood (not that much blood), sweat (a decent amount of sweat), and tears (so many tears) to get there.

————

If making some big changes in your life sounds terrifying, I hear you. I shake in my size 11 boots every time I make a big change, and it's super scary for my coaching clients too. Change, ahhhh! But growing up into who you will be next can also be a lot of fun, and the ability to learn, change, and try something new is a gift not to be squandered in this life, for your own sake and for the benefit of others who will get to enjoy what you uniquely bring to the world.

To work through this together - teamwork makes the dream work - here's what we're going to do. The chapters that follow each focus on a different career development framework or concept but in a fun way. Each topic is rooted in the parenting lessons we teach our children, like using your words, try your best, follow the rules, and money doesn't grow on trees. As I figured out who I wanted to be next, I needed a big reminder about these lessons as much as anyone.

We're also going to be laughing a lot in this book. You might even forget you're learning about how to build your career because you'll be too busy chuckling along with funny and relatable stories about parenthood that will remind you you're not alone. Whether you are working full-time, working part-time, working in the office, working from home, or working inside the home, this motherhood business is bananas. We could all benefit from finding the humor in the hard, taking ourselves less seriously, and laughing until our sides hurt before sitting down to write a job application.

I hope you'll close this book feeling like you've learned something about yourself and that you know how to define what success looks like to you. I hope you'll spend time thinking about how to make your mark and build a fulfilling career and that you'll know how to take action to get there. My other, and perhaps equally important, hope is that you'll laugh out loud in a public place while reading this. I love it when people do that.

Shall we get started? Let's do this. I kicked this project off by asking myself a big question, and I'll ask you now too. *Mommy, what do you want to be when you grow up?*

PART I

FIGURING IT OUT

To get where you're going,
the first step is deciding where it is you want to go.

1

WHAT DO YOU WANT TO BE WHEN YOU GROW UP?

"Jack, what do you want to be when you grow up?"
"A firefighter or a doctor."
"That's awesome, buddy! What do you think Norah is going
to be when she grows up?"
(Thoughtful pause)
"Batman."

*M*y kids, Jack and Norah, are fifteen months apart. I love that they are so close in age because they play together, look out for each other, and sometimes live in their own little sibling world. It's also pretty challenging because when they were babies, they were both babies and then toddlers and then preschoolers who wanted the same toy.

Their age gap is also a great conversation starter with strangers at the grocery store, as it turns out. When I was pregnant with Norah, nearly every grocery store encounter went like this:

"Oh, your baby is so cute! How old is he? And you're

expecting? Wow...You're going to have your hands full. Was that planned? Do you know how procreation works?"

I'm barely embellishing for the sake of the story. People were all up in my business about baby-making, in a fun way that only women get to experience. Perhaps this was because it was barely medically probable that I was growing another human shortly after birthing one. However, some quick math and my children's existence will tell you that yes, it is possible. In general, I'm all for curiosity, and my kids have taught me to double down on that stance, but it's a good idea to keep curiosity out of a stranger's reproductive organs and bedrooms. Save your grocery store questions for the produce guy and focus on the freshness of the kiwis.

The fact of the matter is my husband, Glen, and I suffered three miscarriages before Jack was born, and while we wanted to expand our family, we didn't know if any more children would be in the cards for us. I was constantly afraid of another miscarriage during my entire pregnancy, and it didn't subside afterward. As a result, when Glen and I found out I was pregnant with Norah when Jack was just six months old, we were nervous, but we were beyond ecstatic after seeing her tiny heartbeat. It would be tough parenting a newborn and a toddler, but creating this family was a dream come true.

Grocery store strangers never heard that whole backstory, though. Mostly because I don't like the grocery store, and I wanted to get out of there with my cart of avocados, milk, and comfort chocolate chips as soon as possible. It was also because that might have been a little much to share in the middle of a Trader Joe's. Instead, during the pregnancy and two under two stages, I would nervously laugh and say, "Oh yeah...we'll be fine," as I tried to convince my children to stay in the cart instead of dismantling the cereal aisle.

Fast forward several years, and now I'm more prepared to tackle the age gap question when faced with strangers who want to discuss family planning. The short answer is yes, my hands are quite full, but that's an amazing thing because being a mother was a massive part of what I wanted to be when I grew up. Through all of the career confusion I went through in childhood and into adulthood, motherhood was a constant. On top of all that, raising these two little people inspires me to figure out what I want to be when I grow up next. Every single day.

———

Adults love asking kids, "What do you want to be when you grow up?"

It's super cute to think of little humans being doctors, firefighters, or Batman, so it's entertaining for us. Plus, there is so much value in the "What do you want to be when you grow up?" question from the developmental perspective. Inspiring big dreams, making kids aware of all the options, and encouraging them to create brand new options is excellent parenting. We should keep asking this question all the time!

Yet, we don't. At some point along the way, we stop asking kids "What do you want to be when you grow up?" and we stop asking ourselves too. It's like there's this imaginary line between not grown up and grown up where it seems like all the choices have been made and the dreams need to be reined in.

Of course, as we get older, our responsibilities start piling up higher than the laundry, and we don't have the same freedom to play pretend as we did when we were kids. However, I have yet to find a reliable source that says at what age you need to stop dreaming. What I've learned as a career coach is that if you still kind of want to be an astronaut or a Broadway star when you grow up, there's a way to honor that into adulthood. Maybe you won't be putting on a spacesuit or putting on the Ritz, but you can still find ways to do work you love by thinking about why those specific dreams sound so exciting to you. The process is a bit like being a detective, uncovering clues about yourself, and then fitting the pieces of the puzzle together.

To show you how this career exercise works, come along on a little self-reflection adventure with me as I rewind my career story to 1989, back to when I was a kid with self-cut bangs and big dreams.

———

In the late '80s, I was a four-year-old with a mom, a dad, a baby brother, My Little Pony underwear, and dreams of being an artist. I loved to color and would sometimes draw my masterpieces on paper, but perhaps more commonly, and much to my parents' chagrin, my crayons found their canvas on the radiator.

As we made our way into the mid-'90s, I decided that I wanted to be a food decorator when I grew up. (We went to a fancy restaurant one time and I thought the sauce on the plates looked pretty.) My parents' response to this was, "Becca, I think you might mean 'be a chef.' You would probably also be cooking the food if you were decorating it. Have you thought about being a chef?"

Given my vast experience melting the counter while making macaroni and cheese and closing up a not-fully-popped bag of popcorn WITH A PEN and putting it BACK

IN THE MICROWAVE, I decided to abandon that career path.

From there, my "when I grow up" dreams included novelty key-chain store owner, singer-songwriter, host of Nickelodeon's "Guts," and Zenon: Girl of the 21st Century. The next career idea stuck around for a while, though. I wanted to work in sports. As a multi-sport athlete of medium level skill growing up in a household of sports enthusiasts, I thought this seemed like a natural fit. I also knew one person who went to college for sports marketing and decided that since I liked sports and making posters for Homecoming dances, I had found my calling. At 18, I packed up my My Little Pony underwear and went to Boston College where I studied marketing, cried through every finance assignment, and interned with the Athletics Department.

As a Sports Marketing intern, my role was "make sure kids don't fall out of the bounce house at the alumni tailgate party," which I was quite good at. This child wrangling skill also came in handy in my summer job as a camp counselor, where I taught preteens how to play Four Square, make new friends, and write their resumes so they could be camp counselors one day. This should have been a major sign of things to come, but apparently, I was too busy inexplicably still crimping my hair well into the 2000s, so I didn't notice.

After college, I was offered a nine-month employment contract in the Boston Celtics ticket sales department. While the Celtics were one of the most storied franchises in the history of sports, it had been a tough couple of decades for the team, and season tickets were a hard sell. The little crew of other eager work in sports beavers I joined needed to get on the phone and make some cold calls to fill those seats. At first, the sales calls out to Celtics fans were stressful, but when I learned that sales was all about getting to know people, I ended up having a lot of fun. My days were filled with lots of friendly conversations with people I didn't know about their favorite players, kid's birthday parties, good smoothie recipes, upcoming medical procedures... Fielding inappropriate questions about my sex life in the dairy aisle and then changing my life based on a conversation with a stranger at the DMV suddenly seems much more in character for me than I thought now that I reflect.

A couple of months into my new job, I had made some sales and was hanging in there, by a very precarious "this job pays based on commission" Ramen-filled thread, but I was hanging in there. Then one day in late July 2007, I showed up to work, and there was a buzz in the air. Kevin Garnett was going to be joining the Celtics soon, and our cold calls to sell tickets were about to get a lot easier. Kevin Garnett is very tall and very good at basketball for anyone reading who is not a sports fan. Like he's Beyoncé good at basketball. As a result, the phone started ringing off the hook, tickets were flying out the door, and I made enough money to pay my rent, put a small down payment on a little green Corolla, and bought some more Ramen. Ramen is delicious.

My run at the Celtics was a lot of fun while it lasted, but when my contract was up in February 2008, and all the tickets had been sold, I was given a firm handshake and a box for my belongings. No hard feelings, but now what? I had just spent four years pursuing a degree to land this exact job, and it was gone. Did I need to completely rethink what I wanted to be when I grew up? That wasn't part of the plan! I was supposed to have already done that. What was I going to do now? Go decorate food? I'm not any good at that!

After spiraling and feeling sorry for myself for a reasonable amount of time, I decided to focus on working in college sports since Boston is overflowing with universities. However, it wasn't overflowing with sports positions that wanted to hire me. Instead, I used my marketing degree and minimal sales experience to find a home at Harvard Business School, filling seats in Executive Education classrooms instead of stadiums. As it turned out, while I hadn't thought much about a career in education, I loved working at a university and being part of helping others learn and grow. It felt like being a camp counselor again without the face paint and lawn games. Unfortunately, when I was 17, I didn't know anyone who had majored in camp counseling, and my very short stint as a third-grade substitute teacher did not go well, so I hadn't put this option on the table.

As I built my career at Harvard, I earned a Master's Degree in Higher Education and remembered that I liked helping those preteens write their resumes back in the day. My new degree, a new direction, and new connections led me to a new job in the Harvard Business School Career & Professional Development department. I found my career fit in career services, and nine years flew by as I was promoted from Recruiter Coordinator to Manager, Assistant Director to Associate Director. Initially, my work focused on event planning, but I also got to work with students and the career coaches in our office. I quickly became fascinated with the idea of career coaching because it was this cross between counselor, cheerleader, and storyteller, and at its core, the work was all about helping people live their best lives. With another new goal in sight, I started an intensive five-year process of learning how to be a great career coach and loved every minute of it.

Then came my rookie year as a mom, meeting Kenzie, cheating on my love of career coaching with an equally powerful love of the written word, and some resurfaced nostalgia for my youth. But we've already covered that unless you want me to talk more about Jonathan Taylor Thomas and 90s hairstyles? No? Okay, that's fine. Do you think crimping will come back, though? I still have my crimper, just in case.

————

To recap, throughout my life I have wanted to be a mom, an artist, a food decorator, Zenon, a camp counselor, a marketer, a salesperson, a higher education administrator, a career coach, and now a writer. On the surface, it feels like a weird list of entirely unrelated jobs. However, because of my coach training and the 100 Jobs Exercise from Dr. Tim Butler's book *Getting Unstuck* [1], I learned that everyone has critical themes that run through their life. In the 100 Jobs Exercise, you look at a list of 100 jobs and then quickly circle 12 that sound cool to you. Then you try to figure out why you are attracted to those jobs and what they may have in common. For example, if you picked firefighter, doctor, and school principal, it might be because you love to help people and you like being in positions of authority.

When I tried this same process with my "what I wanted to be" and "what I did" throughout my life and career, I found some themes that created a picture of what I liked to do: creativity, establishing relationships, and problem-solving. Beyond a specific role, organization, or industry, these themes were "my thing." Creativity showed up in art, food decorating, and writing. Relationships showed up in being a camp counselor, higher education administrator, salesperson, and coach. Problem-solving was there in coaching, sales, higher education, and marketing. Motherhood checked off all these boxes too! In each of my jobs and each of my aspirations, even if they were wildly different from one another, there was something I genuinely loved and should continue to build on.

In addition to these core three themes, I also found that I liked to be in control, I enjoyed being scrappy to get things done, and I wanted humor to be central to my life. My job at Harvard was objectively great, but it didn't check off as many boxes as I wanted and I realized it would be a mistake to settle for a career that wasn't a perfect fit because I thought now that I was in my 30s and a mom, I had already made all of my career decisions. For my sake and my kids' sake, I should be striving to honor all of my themes as much as possible, respect my childhood aspirations, and keep dreaming big dreams about the type of life that makes me want to put my hands up and "Shout!" I wanted that kind of happiness for myself, and I also wanted to show my kids that changing, evolving, and finding new dreams to chase is all part of this grand life adventure, whether you are six, thirty-six, or eighty-six.

———

I know that technically I'm a grown-up and you are too, but I don't consider any of us all the way grown-up. I still plan on doing a lot more growing up over the next 60 years or so. Seventy if I start remembering to take my multivitamin. So over these next however many years we have left, let's keep on creating ourselves along the way. That imaginary grown-up line is just that, imaginary. Career development doesn't stop in our 30s, 40s, or beyond. This process of getting curious enough to uncover themes of our past, analyzing what matters most to us, and figuring out what we enjoy in this world can go on for as long as we want to stay engaged with it. Why not start right now?

Before you're interrupted by one of your children who has an urgent need for applesauce, take some time now to reflect on what you have done in your career so far. You can use the notes page at the end of this chapter to make yourself a list of your past and current jobs and then write down the specific parts of those jobs that have given you energy instead of sucking it out of you. This is the "Put your hands up and Shout!" stuff I was talking about. Paychecks are incredibly important, and we aren't going to ignore that we get jobs to make money. However, even if you aren't jazzed about your job right now, there was something else that landed you in this role instead of being an ambulance technician, an acrobat, or an architect. Try to identify what that is.

Go a step further and think about what you wanted to be when you grew up. Did your career turn out that way, or does that dream sound bizarre now? Is your dream career pretty far removed from your reality, but it still sounds kind of appealing? After thinking about all this and jotting down some notes, please call me and tell me all about your childhood dreams and career themes because I'm inquisitive and quite nosy.

If my phone goes to voicemail, bring it up at your dinner table after getting your kid to eat his squash. Get your partner's input on what you've done so far in your career and what you always wanted to be, and see what themes they pick up on. Turn the question over to them too! What did your partner want to be when they grew up? Does it connect in any way to what they do now or the kind of jobs they think sound cool? Get your career coaching on and learn a little bit more about each other. I realize that I'm a career nerd, and my idea of a riveting dinner conversation about career hopes and dreams may not be your jam, but humor me. I think you'll have fun.

While we're on the topic, go ahead and ask your kids what they want to be when they grow up. If your kids are anything like my daughter, Norah, you might get a good chuckle when they reply, "A duck." Or your heart might swell with pride as they discuss how they are going to save the animals or help sick kids. You could be surprised that they have an interest in art, or science, or Olympic curling! Maybe someday you'll be on one of those Olympics commercials about thanking mom!

Perhaps you could even take this question on the road and ask that pregnant lady in aisle eight what she wants to be when she grows up. Trust me; she'll just be glad you didn't ask her if she's having twins.

CHAPTER 1 NOTES

What did you want to be when you grew up?

Think back over your childhood through today. What jobs have sounded exciting to you over the years?

What jobs have you had up to this point?

Don't start at your first job out of school. Include all of your jobs on this list going back as far as you remember.

What common themes do you see among your different dreams and jobs?

(i.e. helping others, leadership, working with animals, teamwork, solo work, creativity, problem-solving, research, being outside, etc.)

YOU NEED TO SHARE

*H*ow many times each day do we use the word "share" as parents? Speaking for myself, it's at least 2.1 million.

"Jack, please share with your sister.
Those Hot Wheels cars are for everyone."

"Norah, it's time to share the yellow marker...now."

"What do you mean I can't have one of your chocolate-covered yogurt raisins? I bought them. Please share."

To ensure that my kids learn how to share, I am often placed in the role of judge, jury, and setter of the kitchen timer. One particular morning at a very early hour, Jack and Norah approached the bench to see The Honorable Mommy with a sharing disagreement that simply had to be pushed up on the docket. Norah had found a yellow rubber bracelet on Jack's bureau, and everyone who had been within a 30-mile radius of Norah at age three knew it was currently her favorite color. She was beaming and admiring her latest find, which was made only better by the fact that she found it in her big brother's room. Jack, on the other hand, was horrified.

Now mind you, he hadn't looked at this bracelet since he got it in a birthday goody bag four months prior. I assure you he had no idea it was even there, but the fact that it was on his sister's wrist was a shock to the system. He lost it and started whining, making demands, and talking about how special the bracelet was to him.

Channeling my best "I just read an article about good parenting and I want to implement what I've learned" voice, I calmly turned to Jack. Then I asked, "Is wearing a yellow rubber bracelet you had forgotten about more important than your sister's happiness?" I realized that I might have gone over his head the moment I said it, but he nodded a solemn "No" and chilled out immediately. Hmmm...we might be onto something here.

———

Sharing is a tricky lesson for kids, and it's a weird one to teach too. If another mom at the park asked to share my phone so she could play Candy Crush, I wouldn't be happily handing it over. If I was in the middle of typing out a sentence and Glen asked to share my computer to comparison shop doormats, I'm sure I'd start muttering that my Word documents are "special to me." So when our kids have to watch someone else play with their Tonka Truck for a few minutes, I understand that it doesn't feel great.

However, we all know that teaching kids to share is critical so they grow up to be adults who donate to charities, volunteer their time, and give blood. That's the kind of sharing you do all the time because you've grown up to be a sharing rock star. Nine gold stars for you! Yet, even if we are good at sharing a bite, or nine, of our desserts with our kids, adults can still be a little stingy when it comes to sharing our authentic selves. That kind of sharing is a lot harder because, along the way, we've filled up our bellies with too much humble pie and too many fear biscuits.

(In case you're wondering, fear biscuits is not a term you should know. I made that up right now with the hopes that it will stick. Pass it on.)

Our humility and fear stop us from sharing what we can uniquely bring to the world because there is a thin line between confidence and being viewed as braggy. We don't want to walk around with others saying, "Woah, she sure thinks she's all that and a bag of chips." Instead, in general, we are more comfortable blending in, eating our pie and biscuits, and keeping the truly unique stuff bottled up.

That's why kids don't like to share if you think about it. Not the pie part, but the scary part. They are scared they are not going to get their yellow rubber bracelet back. They are scared that more for someone else means less for them. They are afraid of losing something super important to them. Adults are a bit more willing to share a pen with a colleague because they are sure they will get the pen back, and if not, there are more in the supply closet. However, they are less willing to share the special parts of themselves because it's scary to think about putting yourself out there and not being able to take it back if you wanted.

Even though it's scary, I push the "share your talents and skills" point in coaching conversations with students, friends, and clients all the time. Yet, as I coached myself through the "when I grow up" process, I realized I wasn't listening to my own advice. Yikes!

While I was building a successful career in higher education and having fun writing my blog, it turns out I wasn't sharing the good stuff. The skills, experiences, and inherent personality traits that lit me up and made me unique and could bring others joy. I kept my funny bone and humor writing away from my professional life for fear of looking silly. Simultaneously, I was scared to talk about career development on my blog because maybe I wouldn't be taken seriously. I shied away from making more time for career coaching in my busy schedule because "my plate was already full." I didn't explore other writing opportunities because I should probably stay in my mom-humor lane. Not sharing the funny pieces or the nerdy pieces of me, it was kind of selfish if I thought about it.

As I tried to figure out how to play nice in the adult sandbox and share my real self with others, I came across the Career Sweet Spot model of career development that I've since adopted and adjusted over the years as I work with my career coaching clients. The model was a perfect and straightforward kick in the "you need to share" pants and it has changed the game for me and so many others.

———

To find your Career Sweet Spot, picture a Venn diagram with three circles or pies if that imagery is still stuck in your head and making you hungry, and the sweet spot is the overlap between your skills, your passions, and the value you bring to others. Put another way, it's about sharing what you're good at, sharing what you love, and sharing your expertise with the world around you.

As we talk through each circle of the Career Sweet Spot, keep in mind that there is a notes section at the end of this chapter to help you capture your thoughts. Or can write down answers in your phone, in a journal, or on the back of a CVS receipt. Honestly, as long as you're writing, we're good.

We'll start with skills, and this one is very straightforward - what are you good at? If your mind immediately goes to book knowledge or work experience, that's an excellent place to start, and it's what I did too when I thought about my skills. I was a marketing and communications major in college, so I'm good at well, communicating. I have a degree in higher education and work in career services, so I know a lot about career development and the job search process. If you were an accounting major, you might be very good with numbers (and I'm incredibly jealous.) As a lawyer, you likely know the ins and out of a courtroom, a contract, and the plot holes of Law & Order. Those are all well-developed and well-earned strengths. Then, of course, it's essential to note your natural talents and street smarts. Are you the hostess with the mostest always throwing incredible parties for your friends? Are you an active listener? Can you run a marathon, start a campfire, or make mac and cheese without referencing the back of the box? These are all skills that make you, you!

If you're ready to give this a try, start making a list of your skills, and don't be shy about it. This can be a long list! Just because no one is paying you $45 million to tell jokes doesn't mean you aren't funny. If your current job doesn't require your creative juices, that doesn't mean they aren't flowing. Give yourself some credit. Write all your skills down, whether you're using them all the time or not. When I did this full exercise, I included everything from complex problem solving and empathy to baking a mean chocolate chip cookie from scratch. There were also some weird things on the list, like having an incredible memory for boy band song lyrics and reaching things out of tall cabinets.

Our next circle in the Career Sweet Spot model is passions. Some passions are going to roll right off your tongue. For me, the easy one was family; it's on my passion list because it's where my heart is. Maybe family is up near the top for you too, and you are also passionate about your faith, your community, or your sports team. Or you could be passionate about world cultures, art, or fitness; if this is easy for you – awesome. These passions will get written right down on your list.

Yet sometimes, the word "passion" feels too heavy. I mean, I like things, but am I "passionate" about them? So if you're in the "what is my passion, let alone plural passions?" camp, let's try something different. Make a list of all the things you ENJOY. All of them. Yup, I'm talking about putting "watching Real Housewives" on your list. I'm saying put "singing in the shower" on your list. Don't hold back or be embarrassed; this isn't your passion list yet. On my list of things I like, I wrote down Twitter, cozy blankets, making my kids laugh, standup comedy, strong female leads in sitcoms, singer-songwriters, and mint chocolate chip ice cream. So, if you are looking for permission to start broad and weird – granted!

Now take a second pass at your list, and without any judgment, let's go back to our trusty theme detective process and try to pull out some commonalities. Love watching The Bachelorette, reading the Skimm, and texting your friends? Why do you like those things? Maybe a theme here is that you want to feel connected with others. Talking about the show the next day at work, reading news highlights, and catching up with your friends helps you do that. Maybe it's that you love the live-tweeting audience of The Bachelorette, appreciate the funny movie quote subject lines of the Skimm, and like hearing your friend's latest hilarious story about the time she tried goat yoga. The theme here? Humor!

Try to come up with several themes that tie together a few of your interests, and there's the start of your passion list. Remember that some of your passions may be lifelong, and others will change over the years, but we're looking for your here and now Sweet Spot knowing that might shift later on. The themes that bubbled to the top of my "things I like" list were laughter, a sense of home, writing, creativity, problem-solving, and mint chocolate chip ice cream... That one didn't fit neatly into a bucket. Or maybe it would fit perfectly into a bucket... With two spoons, I'll share.

We're getting to the secret sauce now, y'all. What you're good at is important. What you love doing is important. When you combine those two things, then you get close to the Sweet Spot. But the value to others is where you get to double down on the sharing, and you aren't going to be giving up anything to do it. You're going to be gaining even more than you give.

Let's say you are a stay-at-home parent considering taking on a job outside the home, but you don't know how your experience translates. In the time you've spent with your kids, you know all the ins and outs of cloth diapers, researching preschools, or navigating food allergies. Maybe you found a great way to convince your kids to eat their vegetables or have been to every playground in a 20-mile radius. You can multitask like a boss, balance a budget, orga-nize a fundraiser, and listen intently. Think of how much value you add to your family's life. Think about how much value you can add to new parents in your area, a local busi-ness trying to attract families with young kids, or a company that needs someone who can keep all of the balls in the air. So. Much. Value!

A person can add value by making others feel comfort-able, sharing their knowledge, offering a service, building a product, or asking the right questions. In all of those examples, you are sharing a part of yourself with the world so that everyone else can benefit from what you bring to the table. Plus, people will pay you to do those skills which takes the overlap between your passions and skills from a hobby to a career.

Coming back to me being self-involved and using myself as an example, on my list of "value to others," I wrote down that I thought I could help other moms managing career and family, people who are unhappy in their jobs, college career services departments, companies that need writing help, and organizations that support working mothers. When Jack did this exercise at 6 AM, his list included his little sister and his mother, who would no longer need to referee this rubber bracelet argument.

Get your note-taking tools of choice out again and make a list of the people or types of organizations you would be able to help. Creating your list of "value to others" might take a little longer, but if you push yourself, you can come up with a list of who you can share with to increase their happiness, success, or well-being.

Now that you know your skills, passions, and value to others, the next step is finding the overlap, The Career Sweet Spot. This is where it feels like your worlds are colliding, and you can get into a flow. The work you do is challenging, but in a way that gets you fired up because it's rooted in your passions, what you know you're good at, and contributing something to other people.

When I found my own Career Sweet Spot in the intersection of writing, relationships, humor, careers, and parenthood, it was a "Holy smokes, Becca Carnahan, this is your life!" moment.

I could do what I loved to do, make a positive impact on

the world, and make an income doing it. I could integrate career development into my parenting humor blog in a fun way and then turn that into a business by taking on advertisers and offering coaching services and products. Since

I loved writing and coaching and loved the people I was helping, I was happy to get up at Way Too Early o'clock to fit in this work while I was still in side hustle mode. Now all of the things I love are my full-time job. Wow...that's good stuff right there. I want that good stuff for you too, for your benefit but also my own. And for everyone else's. If people aren't willing to share their gifts, we all live in Boring Town, USA.

Every day I benefit from someone brave enough to share a part of themselves – on the radio, in books, in the office, at my kids' swim class, in a lab somewhere in Missouri. These people don't know how the world will react to them sharing their talents and ideas, but they put them out there anyway for the rest of us to question, judge, ignore, or love.

The creativity, empathy, ingenuity, and enthusiasm these people so courageously share with those around them keeps us all moving forward and paints our world with new colors. It's inspiring, but when you think about it, it's also vital. The more Career Sweet Spots found, the better off we all are. It's science.

———

While we are talking about sharing, are you ready for an overshare? I'm lactose intolerant. You didn't need to know that, but there it is. I shared. I should also share that I find that most good things in life begin and end with cheese despite this. And subsequently, some painful stomach cramps if I forget to pop a Lactaid pill. But still, all hail the cheese. It's because I enjoy cheese that the wrap up to this chapter makes me so happy. That'll make sense soon. Stick with me.

Fifteen minutes before my alarm went off one very early morning in November 2018, Jack came into my bedroom to ask for some cheese. It was not cheese o'clock. It was be-in-your-bed-still o'clock. I begrudgingly went downstairs to get him some cheese though because my little guy was on a serious growth spurt. I swear he had grown three and a half feet in the past two days. He had also recently requested "a whole cheese pizza just for him," which made my 90s heart soar with the Home Alone reference and made me pat my wallet looking for more cash.

I got Jack the cheese, and then he went back to his bedroom to play with his cars for a little while. Another fifteen minutes later, as I tried to squeeze 1,000 words for this book into my morning, Jack came back into the room and asked if he could help me write. My thoughts immediately went to Jennifer Fulweiler's book, *One Beautiful Dream*.[1]

In *One Beautiful Dream*, Jennifer documents her experience writing her first book while being pregnant several times and homeschooling her six children. The part I loved the most from her book was when she talked about how we never find a perfect work-life balance as moms, but we can find ways to integrate the areas of our lives. She illustrates this by telling the story of when she was on a tight deadline for finishing a chapter in her book, didn't have childcare available, and had a toddler who would not be appeased by sitting in the playpen.

To solve the problem, Jennifer piled her family into the van, parked in random locations around town, and the older kids helped entertain the toddler with a game of eye spy in the backseat while she typed. This wasn't the easiest way to write, but it was the way that worked for her and her kids, and this shared experience helped her write one of her favorite chapters. Then Jennifer took that lesson of sharing an adventure with her kids and shared it with her readers so that other moms could take a pause and say, "Hmm, how is motherhood helping me achieve my goals, rather than holding me back?" That's a great share!

As I write this chapter, Jack is leaning on my arm asking what numbers I am typing and waiting sort of patiently for his chance to share my computer and use Microsoft paint. He knows about my writing adventure because I've told him all about it. We've clinked our glasses over breakfast when I've finished a chapter. We've broken a silly weekday rule and had cookies after dinner because I had an article published by a big website. When he hears about people being writers, he turns to me and says, "Like you, Mom." Dang...

I'm glad I've shared this experience with my kids. I'm glad I shared this itch of creativity at all instead of pushing it down because I assumed my time for career change had passed. I would have missed out on a lot... Then on top of all that, Jack coming in asking if he could help me write was my little guy offering to share a piece of himself. Sort of... He also just wanted to share my computer. However, his act of wanting some cheese and wanted to share led to me finding the right words to wrap up this chapter. Thanks for sharing, bud!

Also, Norah just walked into the room wearing nothing but a diaper and her purple snow boots... so I think this chapter also found itself a not-so-natural ending. But remember, you need to share. Not to be too dramatic about it, but the world needs you to.

CHAPTER 2 NOTES

Skills

What are you good at? On this list include your formal education, on the job training, hobbies you're good at, what makes you a great partner/parent/friend, and more! Make yourself think about it for at least 5 minutes.

Passions

What do you love? If "passion" feels too heavy, start with your interests and look for key themes among them like you did with your jobs in Chapter 1. For example, if you like social media, watching reality dating shows, and spending time with friends, a theme might be that you are passionate about building relationships.

Value to Others

Who can you help? Think about the people you already make a positive impact on in your daily life. Who comes to you for guidance or advice? Who else could benefit from your strengths and experience?

The Career Sweet Spot

Do you see an overlap between what you're able to do (as an employee or entrepreneur) because of your strengths, what people need out in the world, and what you love?

3
———

TRY YOUR BEST

"Jack, why are you sad?"
"Daddy goes fast on his bike.
I want to be faster than Daddy."
"Well, how do you think you'll get faster than Daddy?
By practicing riding your bike or sitting there?"
"Sitting here."

*N*ot exactly the answer I was hoping for. As it turns out, I had some work to do on instilling the "try your best" lesson in my children, just like my parents had to do for me.

My clearest memory of a "try your best" conversation was from when I was a 15-year-old who felt very sorry for herself after getting cut from the varsity soccer team. Should I have made that team? Absolutely not. Leading up to soccer tryouts, I spent plenty of time laying around by the pool with my friends, but zero time practicing soccer. I did run a little with my parents' encouragement but I also complained loudly every single step. To be fair, my dad would do that gross gargle-up-some-phlegm-and-spit thing A LOT when we would run together and it made me gag, but still.

When the team roster was announced without my name on it, I threw myself a pity party. Why wasn't the thing I wanted simply given to me? Why couldn't I ride my bike as fast as Daddy by sitting here? My mom, whom I affectionately call "Merm," nailed the parental response. She said, "I'm sorry you feel that way. You'll just need to try harder next time. You have to put in the work to get what you want." That's some Merm tough love for the win right there. It won't be the first time in my life or this book that my mother will be right, either. Stay tuned.

Looking back, I know what the problem was. I wasn't motivated to put in the work for that soccer team because I didn't like soccer. I would hope beyond hope for pouring rain at 2:30 PM so practice would be canceled. I would dream about twisting an ankle to skip running laps. That's not great. What I actually wanted was to be part of a team, wear the soccer jersey, go to the pasta dinners, and spend time with my friends. I was willing to work hard for other things though. My grades, for example. I was, and still am, a huge competitive nerd and no one had to push me to get my homework done as a kid. I wanted straight 'As' across that report card, and I wanted them badly, so I read, typed, highlighted, read some more, and got the job done. When it came to school, I always tried my best.

Fast forward 20 years and now as a parent, I am constantly asking my kids to try their best. A whiny "I can't do it" is the fastest way to drive me up a wall in Casa de Carnahan. I've seen you do the buckles on your car seat, spear a piece of chicken with your fork, and take off that LEGO guy's head. You've got this, guys – try your best! If you genuinely need help I'll help you, but you need to try first.

"Try your best" is also a common refrain as the kids get older and start to show an interest in sports, so this lesson is coming full circle back to soccer. For the kids, and for me.

When Jack and Norah were three and two, Glen and I asked them if they wanted to try playing soccer. Not really knowing what soccer was they nodded and ran off looking for fruit snacks. A few weeks later, geared up in the tiniest, cutest soccer jerseys you ever did see, the kids hit the field and the results were, well...mixed. Norah's soccer practice was designed for toddlers so she happily ran around the field occasionally kicking a ball but also really enjoying the parachute, hula-hoops, and bubbles that were a mainstay of "soccer."

Jack was in the older group and there was a bit more soccer involved than he had hoped. A few times he would have a fantastic day and run around the field. Still, most days a turtle very literally could have beat him in a foot race and he wanted so many water breaks that I think the other parents probably thought we reserved water only for soccer time. Sorry soccer, he just wasn't that into you.

Of course, organized activities for three-year-olds can be challenging as their attention spans are still developing, and you need a strong teacher/coach/magician to wrangle preschoolers into doing anything in unison. However, part of Jack's lack of soccer enthusiasm was the overflowing enthusiasm he had for something else. After soccer practice, we would walk by the adjacent basketball courts, and stopping to watch the big kids play was his highlight of the day. Then he would want to go home and practice basketball on our Little Tikes hoop in the basement for hours. Well, maybe 25 minutes, but that is hours in the world of a toddler parent. We learned that Jack was willing to try his best, but he also wanted to reserve his "try your best" for something he loved. That sounded pretty familiar.

————

"Try your best" may seem like run-of-the-mill advice in parenting and for your professional life. However, focusing your best effort on what you care about most is a different animal. Sure, as an adult you have to do things you don't want to do, and as a mom, you will end up doing things you definitely don't want to do. Like cleaning poop off a rug at 2 AM. That comes with the territory. But as we wrestle with the concept women have inherited over the years, "having it all," we need to define what our personal "all" really is so that we don't find ourselves simply going through the motions on the soccer field of life.

For me, I started struggling with the concept of "having it all" soon after Jack was born. As a new mom, it didn't take long before I wound myself up in a tizzy trying to be all the things to all the people. I was a mother, an employee, a partner, a daughter, a friend, and a human being who needed to remember to drink water. There were only so many hours in the day and only one of me. If I managed to make many of the things work but not all of the things, would that be enough? I needed some help bringing the thoughts whirling around in my head into focus because I didn't know how to physically try my best at everything. Then Norah was born the next year and the whirling picked up speed. I was on a working mother rollercoaster of my own making and I didn't want to get off, but I did want to slow down to figure out where these tracks were taking me.

It took nearly two years to find that slow-down handle though, which made sense because my hands were quite full with diapers, bottles, and babies for a while. If you are reading this while currently living on Diaper Island then, first of all, you're a champion for reading at all right now, and secondly, give yourself some grace. Time to reflect and slow down might come a little later when your kids start developing a sense of "I do it myself" and your hands become more available to you. Even if the "I do it myself" mindset makes leaving the house maddening. "Nope, your shoe doesn't go on that foot. Still the wrong foot. Honey, the shoe goes on your other foot... Well, now it's on the correct foot but the shoe doesn't fit you anymore because we have been sitting here talking about this for 12 years."

What I did with my now available hands and slightly less foggy brain was spend my time writing and learning how to be the best career coach I could be. I didn't know how it all tied together yet, but I knew I loved writing and I loved helping people and wanted to try my best at both. Then one day in a coach training session focused on how our brains work as adults I learned that there was actual science behind this roller coaster feeling my friends and fellow moms were experiencing. My inner nerd rejoiced!

Psychologist, Dr. Daniel Levinson, spent his career researching adult development stages, focusing on the key turning points we face in life. The stage that had me sitting up a little straighter in my chair and nodding like a bobble-head was the Age 30 Transition (ages 28-40) when adults try to figure out their role in society. Leading up to this stage, young adults spend a lot of time exploring possible career paths, building relationships, and making moves to build out a vision for their lives. They are discovering and goal setting and achieving left and right.

Then something big happens. Perhaps the important milestone is marriage, having kids, or a promotion that sets you on a clear career path. Things start moving. Fast! You have responsibilities with a capital R. As a result, reflection and deep evaluation of your goals take a cracker crumb-covered backseat. The focus goes from dreaming big dreams to making sure all your ducks are in a row for the here and now.

My turning point was the kids. These little people I brought into the world were relying on me for safety, security, and snacks. As I worked through the Age 30 transition, I found motherhood had shifted my priorities and I needed to honor that, while at the same time honoring the person inside me who always loved chasing goals. And the person who needed to pay the bills. Just like Levinson said would happen, I hit age 30 and found myself trying to figure out what I was going to be now that I'd grown up.

However, figuring that out wasn't easy to do when one kid was throwing peas and the other one was making a break for it out the front door wearing only underwear and a smile... Also, did we have enough milk? Shoot...that meeting is tomorrow. And so is Silly Sock Day at daycare... Like mothers everywhere, juggling all of these different feelings and responsibilities made it hard to keep my head above water, let alone deeply reflect and figure out where to focus my efforts. Reflection, focus? My plate is already full, don't ask any more of me, you monster!

I realized that a very full plate is even more reason to make reflection a priority though. It's hard to do it all, but it's much harder to do it all when you don't know what you want your role to be, or what "all" is most meaningful to you. Luckily where Levinson leaves off is where a helpful career coaching exercise from Harvard Business School comes in. At Harvard, my fellow career coaches and I often talk to students about creating a list of career and life criteria, which means doing some soul searching and then writing down what matters most to you and what you're willing to try your best for. Despite over a decade of working in the career and professional development field, I had never actually gone through this exercise for myself. When I did, it changed everything and rerouted my career, even though it was just one simple piece of paper with eight sentences.

Ready to think about what's most important to you? I'll walk you through how I tackled writing career and life criteria for myself and how I've worked on it with coaching clients who are managing careers and family. It might sound like an overwhelming task at first, "Oh yes, sure Becca... let me just jot down what gives my life meaning real quick. Can I borrow a pen?" And I agree that it's not as easy as making a grocery list while you're standing in front of your open fridge. But hey, we can do hard things! And this hard thing is going to help you figure out what you want to try your best at. Totally worth the effort.

Plus skip ahead to the end of the chapter and there's a notes page and worksheet for your criteria so we can get this homework kicked off together before nap time is over.

———

First, you're going to see ten lines on the career and life criteria worksheet and while you don't need to fill in every line, your criteria should be around seven to ten sentences. "Why?" you ask aloud curiously. Well, because there is no way there are only three things that matter to you in your work and life. And if you start going crazy and listing out twenty-five top priorities then you are going to take a look back at your list and say "Nope, can't get all that. Might as well throw in the towel and literally go throw in the towels (in the dryer)." We want to keep this list meaningful and relatively simple so that you can focus on it when making decisions.

Now to start writing your criteria. Start by thinking about the life stuff and jot down one-word answers on the notes page to some very nosey questions I'm about to ask you. Starting with where you want to live. Do you need to be close to family/near a body of water/ in a city/ on a farm? If none of that matters to you and you think you could genuinely be happy anywhere then skip that one, but I find that parents especially have some strong feelings about this.

Speaking of the kids, they are going to factor into this too. Big time. What kinds of things do you want to do for and with your children? Do you want to travel the world with them? Coach soccer? Save for college? Do you want to expose them to different learning environments or help them make new friends? I know for sure you've thought about all this and even if you don't know what's for dinner tonight, you do know what kind of parent you want to be. If the parent you want to be is free-range, or organic, or attachment, or traveling circus that's cool. Own it, and then write it down.

Think about other personal connections too. If you have a partner or close friends and family that factor into your decision-making, they will show up on your career and life criteria list. What do you want your relationships with those people to look like? Do you have dreams that you want to accomplish together? How do your career choices impact those people? Or when I mention connections you might be thinking about pets or the houseplants you keep alive and thriving like some kind of magical wizard. (My sad cactus and I beg you to tell us your secrets!) On your brainstorm list write down the names running through your mind, and then go back and think about what's most important to you about those relationships.

Now we'll move from life onto the career side of this exercise. Start the career criteria part by thinking about what "good work" looks like to you? The kind of work you'd look at and say "Wow! That was an awesome hour/two hours/eight hours. So productive. So rewarding. So motivating!" Is it when you are working as part of a team? Or, is the first image that pops into your mind just you and your thoughts typing, number crunching, or painting? Are you in the weeds with the details or setting a strategy from 30,000 feet? These are the type of day-to-day activities that are giving you energy rather than sucking it dry.

Everyone's version of good work is going to look different, and that's 100% okay. You don't poo-poo the fact that one of your kids likes soccer while the other kid is into basketball right? Two different sports with different environments, but they are equally good work. In the same vein, don't tell yourself that you're some kind of odd hermit if your version of good work is working alone. But if you want to call yourself an odd hermit, fine, we'll be odd hermits together (but separately, in our own homes) because for me "good work" looks like typing away about working motherhood while cozied up in a blanket cocoon.

Let's keep it going on the career front. What kind of environment do you want to be in? Do you like to work outside, inside, in an office, in a hospital, in a school? Is travel important to you or are you a happy homebody? Do you like stability or do you want to slide across the floor in your socks with some Risky Business? How about the mission of the company you work for, is that important to you? There are dozens of other questions you can ask yourself in this process, but this should give you a good start. Money is going to come into play here too, so for now write down a rough idea of how much money would meet your needs, or what your financial goals are. We'll break the topic of money down some more in chapter seventeen "Money Doesn't Grow on Trees."

After you have your brainstorming page filled to the brim with important notes about the people, places, and things you love, go back and try to turn those one-word answers or phrases into sentences. Maybe you wrote down "flexibility," but why do you want or need flexibility in your work? Why this matters so much too you will be completely different from why it matters to me or why it matters to Nicole down the street. When you put the "why" on your criteria list it's going to feel more meaningful and give this sticking power. I love a good A+ or gold star, but no one is giving grades out for criteria lists, so it's not cheating if you peek over my shoulder at what I wrote down for my career and life criteria three years ago. See if this sparks some sentence ideas for your list.

Becca's Career and Life Criteria:

1. Help solve problems and make a positive impact on people's lives. I don't need to be working at a non-profit necessarily, but being in a helper role makes me feel most fulfilled.
2. Get my kids off the bus. Be there for soccer/ballet/chess/mathletes. I want the flexibility that allows me to be present for my kids. That will mean I can't be sitting in traffic

every day, and I would much prefer to be sitting in my leggings.

3. Create. Make. Bring about something new. My work needs to be focused on adding something new to the world by tapping into my creativity and using it often so that I stay inspired. And quite honestly, the creating isn't just for me. I want someone else to appreciate it, love it even!

4. Time to collaborate, time to work solo. I need both interpersonal interaction and the time to work independently to be effective and happy.

5. Laugh every day. Live a life centered on silliness, comedy, wit, not taking yourself too seriously, and gratuitous 90s pop culture references. Model the power of humor to my children so they find joy in life.

6. Be a supportive partner who helps my husband achieve his goals in his career and for his life. Work together as a team to support our family financially and emotionally. We have college funds to save for, and Glen's been talking in his sleep about having a lake house someday.

7. I like a bit of competition, even if that is competing against myself. I do my best when I'm setting goals and checking them off a list. I need goals like I need ice cream, which is to say I need them badly.

8. Family > Everything else. Live in a location close to my parents, prioritize visiting family out of state, and make enough money to do that. I need these people, and they need me.

Do you see how it works? The sentences I wrote dug deeper than "family" or "writing" and became like a mission statement filled with the juicy stuff of my life that holds meaning. The stuff that I am going to try my best for because it's all worthwhile to me. When I sat down with my list three years ago, everything came into much clearer focus, and I could see what I wanted to try my best at, and what I was willing to let go.

I wasn't motivated by chasing after a prestigious title, so I shouldn't do it. I also waved a big Elsa style "Let It Go" to the idea that working meant I had to work in an office all the time. Things that seemed important years ago weren't important to me anymore, and maybe they never had been, but I hadn't stopped to think about it.

Even if you and I have a lot in common and we'd have a lot of fun quoting 90's movies together over margaritas, your criteria and life criteria will likely look very different than mine. Your list will be full of your people, your places, your interests, your needs – the non-negotiables that give you a better idea of what you want and where you are willing to make some tradeoffs. Career and life criteria can change over time and likely will, but so much of this is rooted in your values so it's real, powerful, and doggone crucial to how you define success. It's your definition of "having it all!"

We'll be circling back to your career and life criteria list again later so give it a try now (in pencil) if you haven't yet. Then go take a snack break because you have been working hard! Perhaps get a yogurt parfait? Or a giant chocolate chip cookie...Gosh, I'm really hungry.

———

A couple more things before we turn the page on "Try Your Best" and into "Mother Knows Best." Jack did learn that he needs to practice riding his bike if he wants to go fast. Now that he has tried his best he has gotten much faster, and he strongly believes that he will win the biking section of our town's triathlon.

Also, at age four Jack found that he did like soccer and wanted to try again, but he also went to a basketball clinic this summer. And man...you should have seen this kid work at it. Michael Jordan tongue-out-focus and everything!

Norah is going to be trying her best at something interesting to her this fall too, embracing her performance instincts and taking dance classes. I can't wait to see her try her very best at something she loves. Or tell me three weeks into it that she wants to try karate... Either way, the adventure of learning, exploring, and refining to figure out what "having it all" means to us goes on, and I'm glad you've hopped on board to figure it out for yourself too.

CHAPTER 3 NOTES

Brainstorming Page

Career and Life Criteria

Your career and life criteria are about what has meaning for you and what brings you energy and happiness - personal and work-related. Beyond the how or what, also include the where/when/why behind the criteria so that each sentence has deep meaning to you. Reflect back on this list as you evaluate potential opportunities.

Examples:

1) I want the stability of a steady income with full medical benefits so that I can afford to live in ABC city, enjoy cultural activities in the city, and travel to see my family.
2) To be happy at work I need to be surrounded by a team of colleagues I enjoy who will become key parts of my social circle outside of the office. Personal connections are very important to my overall happiness.

1)

2)

3)

4)

5)

6)

7)

8)

9)

10)

MOTHER KNOWS BEST

I understand it would be very cliché to start this chapter by saying it was a dark and stormy night, but I don't want to lie to you. This story is actually set on a dark and stormy night. Also, it was a Tuesday. Approximately 54 degrees if memory serves.

My commute home from Boston had been especially soul-crushing as it usually was when it rained. I sat in bumper-to-bumper traffic for 25 miles battling windshield wipers that I couldn't quite turn to the appropriate rain speed and a growing stomach that was unamused by the apple in my bag. Then I picked up my kids from daycare minutes before the late charges would start kicking in and we went home to engage in an epic mama versus kiddos dinner time battle. Jack didn't want to eat his chicken, Norah didn't want to eat anything, and yet somehow with all of this non-eating, I was still getting up every two minutes to fetch something for someone. More milk, a napkin for the spilled milk, the bathroom light, butter, ketchup, my sanity... My FitBit clocked thirteen minutes of activity during that dinner, which tells you exactly what you need to know about parenthood.

By bedtime, I managed to find some hidden scraps of patience and convince each child to eat the total number of bites equal to their age. Teeth were brushed, pajamas were on, and bedtime stories were read. My adorable children who had driven me up a wall earlier were safe and sound in my house, we were warm and dry, and life was good. I tucked Jack under his Lightning McQueen comforter, kissed his head, and said to him "You know what, buddy? I always wanted to be a mom. It was my dream to be your mommy and raise you and your sister." He looked up at me a little confused and said "Really??? But we never listen..."

That's some solid self-awareness.

———

While Jack made a good and hilarious point, I did always want to be their mom. From the first moment I cradled a Cabbage Patch Kid in my arms and dressed her in corduroy overalls, I knew that mothering would be in my future.

Of course, I didn't quite know what I was getting into because Barbara Jean didn't backtalk when I asked her to eat her carrots, but of all the titles and roles I've held, Mommy is my favorite. Hands down. These two humans I brought into the world are my heart and I'll always be willing to try my best for them. Parenthood is a career path I'm privileged and grateful to be on.

That being said, there are incredibly challenging non-carrot related parts about motherhood I'll readily admit to and that you'll understand. Like when Jack had a meltdown in the middle of a mall in a Denver suburb and I had to surfboard style carry him out of there. Or when Norah picked up her entire plate of avocado enchiladas that I had just spent an hour cooking and threw them into the wild blue yonder. Or any of those times when one of my children acted exactly like childhood me and I felt compelled to call my mother and apologize. I've apologized to my mother a lot over the past several years. I imagine there will be many more apologies in our future.

What I've come to realize is that my mother really did know best when I was a kid. My still-developing frontal cortex may have thought I had it all figured out, but I didn't. Merm had 25 years on me and in those 25 years she picked up quite a few life lessons that I should have been very grateful for. I know that now. One day I'm sure my children will be calling me to apologize when they are arguing with small versions of themselves in a Dunkin Donuts, and that will be a very funny and satisfying day.

If you've also made some apology calls to your mom over the years, you and I both have seen the adage "mother knows best" play out in real life. At the same time, it can be easy to forget that we are the mothers now and we know best for ourselves and our families too. This motherhood learning curve is steep, long, and winding and I know I'm not alone in saying there are times when I feel like I have no idea what I'm doing. Staring down a three-year-old to convince her to take a nap while she laughs in your face can shake your confidence. Plus, as I look ahead to the future of parenthood I have no idea how to handle report cards, teenage grunts, and broken hearts. The anxiety bubble in my throat is building even as I type that! I know I'll figure it out when I get there though. That's what moms do.

———

We aren't going to be using any career frameworks as this Mother Knows Best chapter continues. Go ahead and put away the pens! Instead, as part of the "figuring it out stage" of career development we're simply going to lean into the hard of working motherhood together.

This gig is not easy and a big part of trying to map out what life is going to look like as mommy grows up is taking on the unique challenges working mothers face today. Fathers are much more involved in childcare than in previous generations which is awesome, but still the phrase "working mom" is commonplace, but "working dad," not so much. The pressures placed on women are different in our society even after years and years of women working outside of the home in a wide range of roles. It's all this societal pressure, oversized expectations, and a laundry list of responsibilities that lead to working moms dancing backward in high heels trying to make it all work. I find this especially challenging because I've never been great just walking in heels. Picture an injured baby deer.

One of the first hurdles working mothers face is the idea of going back to work at all after having children. A boat that some of you reading may currently be sailing in. If you have a husband or male partner, how many times has he been asked if he is going back to work after becoming a dad? I would venture to guess a total of zero times unless your family has recently won the lottery or done exceptionally well on a game show. People generally assume that you need money to raise children, which is correct, and jobs are very important for bringing in money. Someone is going to have to have one of those and it's often assumed that person will be a man even if a woman has a very successful career.

I have another question. How many times has your male partner been asked what his plans are for childcare after the baby is born? I'll bump this one up to maybe two times because I'm feeling progressive. However, as soon as a woman starts showing signs of growing a life inside her the questions about going back to work and who is going to take care of the baby start rolling in, and the judgments pile on faster than the pounds. Sometimes the judgment is direct and harsh. Sometimes it's just the perceived judgments because a question from your Great Aunt Mildred about going back to work is intended to be completely innocuous, but you feel the weight of it later that night as you rethink all your life choices and crunch the daycare/nanny/stay home numbers again.

Despite not having won the lottery or done very well on a game show, being a stay-at-home mom was something I thought a lot about before getting pregnant with Jack. My mom stayed home with me and my brother until I was eight years old and was amazing at it. Growing up, I knew many great stay-at-home mothers in my small town and thought perhaps that would be my path too. However, by the time my children came onto the scene going down to one income didn't feel realistic for me and Glen. Plus, after three months of maternity leave, I was looking forward to returning to the office. I didn't know what I was doing as a mom and I missed knowing how to do things. I also missed talking to adults, and I even missed putting on real pants.

So, on Tuesday, May 26, 2015, I went back to work three months after Jack was born. I remember this day vividly for a few reasons, not the least of which are the brutal ugly tears I cried on the way into the office. As I learned, you can miss work and still ugly cry as you drive there that first day; those two things are not mutually exclusive. Vision blurred and already feeling some chafing from office-appropriate footwear, the day did not start well. Then I got into the office and cried some more as I put pictures of my sweet little dude up on the wall. The waterworks continued the first time a coworker dared to say "Becca! Hi!" I was a mess and I knew the tears were coming from two places. One, I missed Jack. He was a very cute baby with very squishable cheeks. Two, I felt horribly guilty for wanting to be at work and eating lunch without being covered in spit-up.

There's that guilt word. You were waiting for it, right? A book about working motherhood and we have gone four chapters without talking about mom guilt? Crazy! If you've never felt mom guilt before I'll break it down.

Mom guilt is that feeling in your mom-gut and heart that you're doing something wrong at every turn. Not giving in to read one more book before bedtime – mom guilt. Giving in to read one more book before bedtime – mom guilt. When your son says that he wants to stay home in his pajamas all day as you're pulling on your blazer for work – mom guilt. I have worried that sending them to daycare so that I could work is selfish. I have worried that not sending them just so one of my kids won't accidentally call me by the teacher's name again would be selfish. As the years go on I harbor mom guilt over organic vegetables, screen time, organized activities, birthday parties, play dough, and outerwear. Sound familiar?

Was the term "mom guilt" even around when we were kids growing up? I googled it and it seems to be a relatively recent term coined for modern parenthood. So that's fun. I'm sure it stems from the ability to constantly compare ourselves against other mothers outside of our neighborhoods through an onslaught of social media. Social media that I willingly participate in to be fair, because social media is fun. I mean, have you seen the memes? It's like comedians are right at your fingertips ready to say "Hey girl, I get you."

But as a result of the comparison game and the information superhighway, mom guilt rides shotgun all the time. Sometimes it sits quietly there, not requesting snacks or anything. So considerate! Sometimes it's loud and needy and changes the radio station and makes me cry in my car.

The only good thing about mom guilt is that other moms understand. Circling back to that first day back to work after maternity leave, on top of all my mom-guilt, I felt like I sort of forgot how to work in an office.

What's my computer password? Do I sign this email "Love, Becca" or is it "Best regards"? What does that acronym mean? Oh, sweet Lord, we're supposed to do math here??? Trying to slip back into my professional identity wasn't as easy as I thought it would be with my mind on my baby and my baby on my mind. Also, I hugged a coworker that day whom I should not have hugged. We weren't that close. It was an instinct since the past three months I had been around other hormonal first-time mothers who all needed hugs. It took about four years but I think my coworker and I are cool now. She's a mom too, she got it.

There was another mom who understood what I was feeling that day and she became my superhero. Super Cathy. Cathy and I worked together at Harvard Business School for three years before her family moved away. Thanks to the glorious internet age we kept in touch by email and the occasional Facebook shout-out. I could always count on Canadian Cathy to help me convert Fahrenheit to Celsius, remind me of Canadian holidays, and to be the ultimate truth-teller. Before I had Jack she was the only one to tell me that I might be really sad after having a baby, and that was okay as long I made sure I talked about my feelings. Have a friend like Cathy, be a Cathy.

As a mom of two, Cathy also knew that the first day back

to work can be tough on the head and the heart. She had gotten to know me quite well over the years and understood that if anything was going to keep me powering through the day it was going to be laughter. So at 8:32 AM that first day back in the office, Cathy sent me this email:

Subject: Question 1

Q: What did one mushroom say to the other mushroom?

A: You're a fun guy.

That was it. No other context. It was perfect. At 10:50 AM, Cathy sent me this email:

Subject: Question 2

Q. Why can't you hear a pterodactyl going to the bathroom?

A. Because the "P" is silent.

This woman had jokes queued up for the entire day. Every two hours a new one would pop into my inbox to keep me smiling and keep me distracted from the guilt. It was her way of reminding me to trust myself without any explicit pep talks and to let me know that someone out there understood what going back to work after maternity leave felt like. The last email of the day was my favorite:

I went to the zoo the other day. It was empty, except for a single dog...

It was a Shih Tzu.

All of those jokes didn't make my mom guilt go away, but they certainly reminded me I was a person separate from my sweet baby boy, and separate from my professional career. I was me, I loved jokes, and I mattered. All that from some one-liners courtesy of a fellow mom who was there for me in the trenches.

———

While we are on the subject of mom guilt, sometimes the judgment we feel as women isn't imagined at all. Sometimes it is very real and of the "let me tell you how to live" variety. Fast forward four years from that first day back in the office and I had settled in somewhat comfortably to my working mom life but was also starting to seriously consider a change because of all the self-reflection and career coaching I was doing. With these thoughts rolling around in my head, I revealed to a woman I didn't know all that well that I was considering making a change when my son went to kindergarten and stepping away from my full-time role at Harvard. She in no uncertain terms told me I would be "throwing my career away." I was dumbfounded. Then I was fired up. "Throwing my career away!" How dare she?

At that moment, I wanted to scream "You don't know my life!" and now more than a year removed from the conversation I want to scream that from the rooftops to help drown out the garbage "throwing away" phrase women hear all the time. Whether it is throwing away our careers, or throwing away time with our kids, it's a bit of dirt kicked up in our faces when someone else puts their judgment on what and who we value. You and only you know how to make the best decision you can make for yourself and your family. No one else can tell you what is best, or what should be valued, or what you should/could/or want to "throw away." It still stings when we hear it though and these words can make it extra difficult to jump back into your career, or step back from your career, or change your career.

Maybe there will come a stage in your life when you reprioritize, refocus, or realign. Or you might rewind, reduce, or reconsider. All of these decisions are deeply personal and you're considering lots of factors in the process, including all those extra voices playing in your head. But as loud as those "throwing away" voices can be, remember that as long as you know who you are and what's important to you, you are not throwing ANYTHING away. You're awesome, just the way you are, and I'll support your choices until the cows come home.

I hope this extremely fired up support is meaningful to you, but at the same time, regardless of how much anyone is building you up to ignore the haters who are going to hate and telling you that you are the bees' knees, I understand that change can feel like a Shih Tzu. Going back to work after three months or three years or a decade can leave you feeling sad, or happy, or confused that you are both sad and happy. Changing jobs or completely switching gears in your career can leave you feeling selfish, or scared, or foolish, or excited, or anxious, or inspired, or all of those things.

However, I know that for me when things get tough I have to keep going knowing that I am the one in charge here. Of my life, my career, and of my decisions as a mother. This mother knows what's best for me. You know what's best for you.

———

Several weeks after Jack made his spot-on observation about listening skills, we had another bedtime conversation that I like to replay in my mind often. I don't remember if it was stormy or dark that night, but I do clearly remember that he turned to me and said: "Mommy, I think you are a beautiful genius."

I've fallen back on this compliment a lot since that night. When I'm struggling with how to approach a difficult conversation, dealing with a complicated career coaching situation, or avoiding setting up the security certificate on my blog because it seems hard, I remind myself that someone thinks I'm a beautiful genius. When I catch a glimpse of myself in the mirror and do a double-take because my hair looks like it's home to a family of blue jays, I remind myself that someone thinks I'm a beautiful genius. When someone questions my choice to be a working mom, or I question my own choice to be a working mom, or I think that all of these balls in the air will come tumbling down, I remind myself that someone thinks I'm a beautiful genius. A very important someone.

I think you're a beautiful genius too. Specifically, you're a beautiful genius who wants what is best for her family and is busting her butt to make it happen. I want to pour that affirmation out into the world and into stressed-out moms' hearts because honestly, we need it.

Our choices as mothers face scrutiny on the daily. From how well our children are dressed, to how well we are dressed, to how clean our houses, cars, or laundry is. Or isn't. That's on top of the career piece of this puzzle, as well as body image, relationships, patience levels, and ability to keep a small child entertained in a long line at Target. Even if the scrutiny we face isn't coming from the outside and is completely self-inflicted, it's there. We put a lot on ourselves to hold it all together and paint a picture of Pinterest perfection to the world. It can all feel very heavy to carry, and if you're feeling unsure of yourself in any area of your life, and you're not feeling like so much of a beautiful genius right now, you aren't alone. Not one bit.

Motherhood + Career = Confusing. It's hard to be your own person when you have children and are thinking about your career, and it's easy to think you are getting everything wrong. Whether you stay at home with your kids or are working outside the home, it's hard to look at yourself in the mirror and consistently see a beautiful genius. It's hard because you have a lot on your plate, it's hard because of societal pressures, it's hard because you don't have time to even look in the mirror it seems.

It's also important though because lady...your happiness matters. Don't let anyone tell you differently. You are a grown woman who has learned a lot in your life, and you're constantly looking to learn more. You're super tired but you're still reading a book for Pete's sake! You're a rockstar! As we press forward with more tactics to help you live your best career life, this is the foundation. Trusting yourself, knowing you matter, believing that you are a beautiful genius. Grab on tight to the notion that you as a mother know best when it comes to your life. The rest of this is just gravy. (But very important, helpful, and delicious gravy.)

CHAPTER 4 NOTES

No homework from me for this chapter! You can write down any reflections you have from Part I, or don't. You're the mom and you know what's best for you.

PART II

MAKING A CHANGE

Starting to feel a little clearer about your direction? Let's talk about how to make it happen.

USE YOUR IMAGINATION

*R*aise your hand if you'd heard one of your kids say "Mom, I'm bored. There's nothing to do!" Now keep that hand up if your kids have said this while standing in the middle of a room surrounded by toys and the words have made you want to levitate in plastic-coated rage.

Don't be shy, your hand isn't up there alone. One of my children, who shall remain nameless, dared to use the word "bored" the day after Christmas. THE DAY AFTER CHRISTMAS. "Nothing fun to do here" was also whispered in hushed tones once when I denied a trip to the park and suggested the kids play with the LEGOS, trains, and kinetic sand that were strewn about our home. The tones were not hushed enough, I heard. Moms always hear. Even when I don't hear I pretend like I heard now, which is a fun trick. "Oh, I heard that" usually sends a child scampering to do a chore or help a sibling. I shouldn't break it out too often though, with great power comes great responsibility.

The boredom fights are especially frustrating because we know our kids have these amazing imaginations to tap into! For example, when my kids are playing with friends it's not uncommon to hear them come up with some bizarre-sounding game like "Cheese Monster Pirate Tag." As I sit here in my adult world, that was the weirdest name for a game that I could even come up with and I thought about it for a while! When I asked Norah to create a name for a game she made up seven new words and then ran off because that stick looked like a dinosaur. See kids - you're crazy creative. Now use those imaginations and go play. Please and thank you!

———

As the kids run off to use their creative genius to finger paint the kitchen cabinets or create booby traps a la Kevin McCallister, they leave us alone with our thoughts for a moment. Kind of unsettling to have a moment of quiet time, right?

As busy moms, our days are filled with lots of words and very little silence, starting with being woken up pre-dawn by a small child three inches from your face requesting water. If you work outside of the home, your day then goes into hyperdrive after that wake-up call. You get kids ready for the day and attempt to clean and clothe yourself.

Then you get yourself to work and put out fires all day at the office. At the "end of the day," you talk to teachers and other parents at daycare or school pick up and answer rapid-fire questions from your kids on the drive home. Over dinner, you talk to your family and shortly thereafter you begin the bedtime negotiations. Eventually, you sink into your couch sometime past 8:00 PM and try to carve out a little conversing time with your spouse before you pass out. That conversation is often about dentist appointments.

If you work inside of the home, your day also goes into

hyperdrive right away. You get older kids off to school via bus or incredibly lengthy and complainy drop-off line and then get younger kids out of the house to an activity so they don't tear your home apart. Then you talk to the younger child the whole way home from the said activity so that she doesn't fall asleep in the car and ruin naptime.

Eventually, you win the battle of naptime, but some days you don't and there is more talking. If naptime is a success you run around like the Tasmanian Devil on Red Bull for an hour and a half trying to take care of all the adult things in your life in an impossible amount of time, and you guessed it... oftentimes there is more talking. Making appointments, paying bills, returning that phone call. Then you're picking up older kids from school and you and the work outside the home mom are on the same path of noise, and joy, and noise.

However, as every expert, celebrity, and Facebook commenter will tell you, silence is important. They won't say silence though, they will say "meditation," which is exactly where they lose me. I barely have time to cut my toenails, when am I going to meditate? This is not to say I dispute the benefits; meditation has positive impacts on our minds by reducing stress and anxiety, is good for our bodies by boosting immunity and heart health, and can improve focus and self-control. I just feel like there are a lot of expectations and commitment that come along with meditation and I already have a laundry list of things to do, seven of which are laundry. Also, it seems kind of boring. But when I read a blog post by Kallie Branciforte on "But First, Coffee" about the benefits of boredom, and the very practical way she found a pocket of silence to tap into her boredom, I was intrigued.

In Branciforte's post, she talked about how as a society,

we have gotten so busy that our creativity is on the decline and our stress is on the rise. When our brains are constantly being bombarded by information, we lose time to reflect, use our imaginations, and make new connections in our brain from existing information.

When I researched this further I learned that 70% of American adults use a second screen (phone or tablet) while watching TV and we spend on average 11 hours a day interacting with media.[1] No wonder we can't use our imaginations like kids do. Our imaginations are full! And I'm not getting all holier than thou on you here, I'm completely, 100% guilty of this. I like to call it multitasking when in reality, it's brain overload.

Branciforte was feeling this overload too and after listening to a TedTalk from Manoush Zomorodi, author of *Bored and Brilliant: How Spacing Out Can Unlock Your Most Productive and Creative Self*[2], she decided to lean into the idea of boredom.

On her way into work in the morning, Branciforte turned off the radio and the podcasts and drove her twenty-minute commute in silence without the additional distractions of other people's thoughts. She used a time in which she would normally be super bored to see if she could unlock the "default mode" of her brain like Zomoradi suggested, rekindle her imagination, and be more creative at work and in her life.

At the time I read this I was parenting two toddlers, working full-time, my entire family wanted to eat dinner every night for some reason, and I fancied myself a Twitter comedian. My entire life was (and still is) one giant multitasking whirlwind. But as I struggled with how to tie the different pieces of my life together to make a change in my career, I knew I needed some time to think and time to get creative about my next steps.

With a bit of skepticism, I decided to follow Branciforte's lead and drive in silence for at least twenty minutes during my hour and a half commute. The results of this simple decision started rolling in fast! As I sat quietly in traffic and let my brain get into default mode, I figured out how to integrate career development into my humor blog.

I was in the car when I mapped out the different revenue streams for my business including career coaching, blogging, writing books, and creating digital products. I also came up with the entire text of my children's book *Belinda Baloney Changes Her Mind* in the car and recorded it using voice memos. Seriously, I wrote a book in the car because I made myself get bored. If you're trying to make a change, this trick works!

Leaning into my fake meditation time in the car works for me, even if it's just the seven-minute drive after dropping the kids off at school, and that might work for you too. Or, instead of pulling out your phone to scroll Instagram when your snuggly baby decides you make a good bed, try just sitting there and be with your thoughts in a stolen moment of quiet. Another way to sneak in some quiet is to leave the headphones at home when you go out for a jog and give yourself some sweaty time to think.

Or when all else fails, go take a shower! There are no distractions in the shower, well at least until a small child comes running in asking you to get her some milk, so it's the perfect time to let your mind wander and start making connections and coming up with ideas. I know, I know. This idea about coming up with good ideas in the shower is so revolutionary. I should start being a spokesperson for showers! Come on down to the shower emporium, people, we're changing lives!

While sitting in the car, jogging down the street, or washing your feet with zero entertainment may seem boring, keep in mind that boredom isn't a bad thing. It forces you to think for yourself thereby sparking your creativity and problem-solving abilities, perhaps leading you down a career path you hadn't considered before. Or giving you a brilliant idea about how to pull together a few of your different interests and fulfill your career and life criteria. And at the very least, giving yourself a little bit of quiet time will reduce your chances of getting a headache and you'll save some Advil for when you really need it. You're welcome in advance.

———

Another way that kids instinctively tap into their creative sides is their ability to be open to new ideas, new people, and new ways of thinking. We tend to get a little stuck in our ways as adults and our imaginations follow suit. But watch how the kids do it and you'll soak in a bit of that magic.

After a particularly bad winter storm, my kids' daycare center had lost electricity and was closed for the day. While Glen managed back to back meetings, I took the morning childcare shift and shuffled the kids out to the nearby children's museum for a couple of hours of exploring in water tables and air tunnels.

As it turned out, that random Tuesday was an awesome day to visit the museum because college students from Japan were there as part of a cultural exchange to teach children about Japanese songs, toys, and customs. Jack and Norah walked into the room filled with young women from a different country speaking a different language, and where adults might get nervous, these kids dove right in. Their open-minded little brains found that you could listen to a book in Japanese and understand what was going on based on the pictures. You could play with traditional Japanese toys and understand how they work through smiles and nods.

After the formal session was done, some of the Japanese students wandered through the museum interacting with the kids at other exhibits. Two of these lovely women found themselves next to my kids at a craft table teaching them how to properly use scissors and decorating cardboard with ribbons and pom-poms. As they played, Jack learned from his new friend that one word for pants in Japanese is also pants, a fact I'm still weirdly blown away by. Jack also ran off with this new friend and didn't tell me where he was going which sent me into a momentary tailspin, but he was fine and that's a story for another time. In any case, pants in Japanese is pants!

I'm grateful for that no power day. Usually, unexpected days off from work stress me out a lot, but by being more open to the possibilities of the day, my kids got to show me what openness is all about it. It's learning, growing, and making new friends. Being open is letting your mind be unrestricted by boundaries that don't exist. Sometimes it can mean an origami cat you cherish forever and a memory etched in your mind about a time your kids showed you the world ten miles from your house.

The lesson here, openness makes things happen. So, if your imagination well is running dry and you are stuck on how to move forward with an idea, a project, or a plan, mix things up! Shonda Rhimes *Year of Yes*[3] your own life and start saying yes to activities you'd normally say no to.

For me, this was going to an Orange Theory exercise class (here's where you're going to need that Advil I had you save earlier), fumbling my way through Intro to Photography, and finally reading Harry Potter, even though I had been adamant for years that I'm not a fan of the fantasy genre. Each of those activities inspired new blog posts that contributed to my growing businesses, and more importantly, each gave me new ways to look at the world. This practice of being open and saying yes can even be as simple as hanging your head off the couch and seeing the world upside down or putting your right foot in and shaking it all about without abandon.

You could also embrace this saying "yes" mentality by agreeing to try ordering something different from the pizza place down the street. Have you ever tried cauliflower on a pizza? Not as a crust, don't be ridiculous, but cauliflower on top of the pizza is delicious!

Cauliflower pizza aside, whenever you're open to new experiences and ways to view the world, creativity sees an opening and sneaks in. And when creativity sneaks in, you start to look at things from a different perspective. It could be a creative solution to a problem you're facing at work that allows you to tap into another part of your brain that's been itching to get out. It could be a better way to tackle the bedtime routine, which will keep your kids in bed at night, leaving you more time to pursue your passions in the evening. Without imagination, openness, and creativity you wouldn't know that awesome fact about Japanese pants! Instead, I would have spent most of this chapter quoting more stats about screen time and putting you to sleep. See? Creativity: it's the secret sauce to making things happen.

———

Time to put all of this "use your imagination" business into practice to help you go from figuring it out to making a change. First things first, try to find your quiet minutes of the day and use them to get a little bored. At the end of this chapter, make a list of a couple of different ways you could find some quiet time in your day and commit to taking advantage of that time to do nothing. Then, use the second column to write down at least three different activities you could try that would push you out of your comfort zone and into a new experience. These two quick exercises might be just the game-changers you need to start making moves and making changes.

But some of you might be tired of writing, and that's okay. There are different ways to tap into your creativity because of course there are. This is the imagination chapter after all! So if you need to come at this making a change stuff from a different angle, put down the pen, pick up the scissors, and start crafting your very own dream board. Or, if "dream board" sounds too hokey to you, we can call it a Visual Diagram of Your Strategic Initiatives, but it still involves glue sticks.

Get your best piece of construction paper and a stack of magazines and cut out images that speak to you and glue them onto a piece of paper. Or do some copy and paste on the computer if your kid has stolen all of the glue sticks and money for magazines. You could even draw your images at the end of the chapter if you're feeling extra artsy. As you're picking images, see what you are drawn to and include items that represent what you want out of life. A beautiful house that you'd like to live in one day? Get it on there. A family spending time together at a park? Add that. A corner office, a dog, a church, money, a partner, a cruise ship, a mountain, a comedy stage, a book? Glue, baby, blue. Draw, baby, draw.

Try not to put limitations on yourself; if something inspires you, don't question it. If you have a dream that seems too big, ignore that nagging feeling. Dream boards, oh excuse me, Visual Diagrams of Your Strategic Initiatives, are effective because pictures give us something very tangible to latch onto and can give you clarity about what motivates you when you're feeling stuck. Once you have your images down, look at them and see how the whole picture makes you feel. Overwhelmed by the things you don't have? Grateful for what you do have? Hopeful? Scared? Excited? Do your images relate to your specified career and life criteria? Or perhaps your images led you to realize there was something big there that is important to you that you need to add to your career and life criteria. Interesting, eh? Then hang that baby up someplace you'll see it often as motivation to keep moving and create a life you love.

When I created my Visual Diagram of Strategic Initiatives a few years back, there were no fancy cars, parties, or caviar on there. In fact, it took me several tries before autocorrect realized I was trying to type caviar just now.

My construction paper had a picture of a house that looks much like my own, my family, a beach, a laptop, a stack of books, people laughing, s'mores, the sun, a thought bubble, a big heart, and a lounge chair. I've realized that my strategic initiatives are rather simple. I want to be with the people I love, doing what I love, where I love, with what I love. I want quiet time, but I also enjoy connecting with people. Nothing earth-shattering here, but it's me in pictures. It's the things, people, and feelings I want to try my best for and what I want to consistently remind myself to try my best for.

I love me some words, but this additional creative outlet gives meaning to the odd adage "a picture is worth a thousand words" because it boils everything done while at the same time speaking volumes. It's like the Tyra Banks' smize. She doesn't even need to say anything, you just know! So, in honor of that, the next two chapters are just going to be selfies of me practicing my smize. Enjoy.

———

One day out of the blue Jack and Norah turned the "use your imagination" tables on me and Glen which was at first a bit mentally exhausting but became a lot of fun. Instead of wanting to hear stories from books, after eating the required four bites of Brussel sprouts, every night after dinner they wanted us to come up with new stories, straight from our brains, and on the spot. We were given a character to work with but the plot was fully Mom and Dad's responsibility. This led to some pretty ridiculous tales about ducks and ducktails. Once there was a firefighter named Rogeroni and his giraffe named Spot, and in my personal favorite from Glen, aliens came to Earth and stole all of the Backstreet Boys' moves.

As this game continues we find ourselves laughing a lot after dinner, sometimes at how wild the stories get, and sometimes at how much our kids are entertained by something that any publisher would deem derivative, uninspired, or simply a chorus of farm animal noises. We also learn a lot from telling these stories. We learn to think way outside of the box. We learn to think outside of the galaxy. We learn to be open, be curious, and make the space for new things.

Imagination is a powerful force. Without it, we walk around like finely tuned robots, and not the fancy kind with feelings. We go through the motions of our lives, sometimes efficiently, sometimes not, and we miss out on a whole potential world of possibilities. If I haven't already given you enough homework in this chapter, try the impromptu dinner table storytelling activity too. Embrace seeing things a little differently and use your childlike imagination to put something out there that may at first be nonsense, or it may be magic. Then use all those creative juices to make something beautiful – your life.

CHAPTER 5 NOTES

Where can you find your quiet time?

What new activities could you say "yes" to?

Visual Diagram of Strategic Initiatives (Vision Board)

Are you a visual person? Use the space below to start sketching out ideas for your vision board. What images come to mind for you as you think about what's next?

USE YOUR WORDS

*I*n terms of my parenting credentials, I'm certified in baby, toddler, and preschool. And by "certified" I mean I once was a baby, a toddler, and a preschooler and I have been moderately successful at navigating those stages for Jack and Norah as their mother. The actual certificate is one I printed from Microsoft Word when I managed to get both a baby and a toddler into a car by myself and deemed this achievement award-worthy.

What this certificate tells me is that while I can't speak to parenting a tween or a teenager, I've been around the toddler block and there is a lot to learn on the toddler block. Like A LOT to learn. Have you ever searched Pinterest for "parenting toddlers"? Try it and your keyboard will instantly burst into flames due to excessive search results. There's an overwhelming amount of information out there about toddler wrangling because they are complicated little creatures who are impossible to put to bed. They also lack command of the English language but have lots of opinions they like to change their minds about mid-opinion. Sometimes they express those opinions with real words, and sometimes they express them with a combination of screeches that could be confused with the nighttime cries of a fisher cat.

One day when Norah was one year old, she and I spent the better part of a morning toe to toe as I incorrectly guessed her needs multiple times and bore the brunt of her tiny toddler wrath. After we both cooled off and she settled in with some Cheerios, for some reason I started singing the Spice Girls song "Wannabe"[1] to myself. One chorus in and I had a light bulb moment. Maybe the Spice Girls wanted us to think the lyrics "really really want" were about friendship or a gentleman caller trying to court one of the ladies Spice. However, when you really listen to the words, Posh, Baby, Scary, Sporty, and Ginger were preparing the youth of the world to be toddler parents and it was downright brilliant. Let's break this one down line by perfect line.

"Yo, I'll tell you what I want, what I really, really want."

Says the toddler, without giving any indication of what it is that she really, really wants.

"So tell me what you want, what you really, really want."

Says the parent. I hear you. You are pointing up at the counter with fervor and your toddler babble is very loud but everything I seem to be handing you is wrong. Goldfish crackers? This toy car? My keys? My sanity? Please tell me what you want, what you really, really want. And maybe use an inside voice.

"I'll tell you what I want, what I really, really want."

Says the toddler. She doesn't know how much clearer she could be. THAT is what she wants and she doesn't only want it right now, she wanted it ten minutes ago and you should have read her mind to know that.

"So tell me what you want, what you really, really want."

Says the parent. I see that you're upset but I have handed you everything on this counter beside the knife block and that's going to be a hard no. Please tell me what you want, what you really, really want. Watch how Mommy uses her words. I really, really want world peace, more companies to adopt family-friendly work policies, and a margarita.

I wanna, (ha) I wanna, (ha) I wanna, (ha) I wanna, (ha)

Says the toddler, now hyperventilating from disappointment, frustration, and a little bit of shangry (sleepy, hungry, and angry.) "You are just the worst. Why are you ruining my life? I thought I was your sunshine, joy, and reason for existence. FOR THE LOVE OF ELMO, PROVE IT!!!!"

I wanna, really, really, really wanna zigazig ah.

Says the toddler, finally. "I want a zigazig ah. See, now I am being perfectly clear! Hand it over, please."

Leaving the parent to say, "But honey, that's not a thing. It's a made-up word. I don't know how to give you a zigazig ah. So please..."

"Tell me what you want, what you really, really want."

It's the classic Spice Girls Toddler Conundrum.

———

We could have skipped the last two pages of Spice Girls lyrics if Norah had simply used her words to tell me she wanted Cheerios. However, she was a tiny toddler so we'll give her a pass, and I do enjoy that the Spice Girls are given some solid real estate in this book. Plus, this whole idea of "use your words" is directly related to our career development as adults too, so the Spice Girls gave us the perfect springboard back into careers.

To make a change and unstick a stuck career, you can't point at a new job and have it handed to you. If you're feeling like you've lost control over where your life is headed, screaming into the abyss might feel good but won't do anything. If this (gestures with open arms around the general area) just isn't working, you have a choice to make. Silently stew in your stress or use your words. At the office, at home, or anywhere we are in between, we can't expect our friends, family, or managers to read our minds.

If you ask Glen, I use plenty of words at home. Arguably more than my fair share. I like to talk out a problem until I'm blue in the face and he's blue from listening to me. However, he does patiently listen because he knows as well as I do that when I don't talk it out, I'll bottle it all up as fuel for the mommy rage monster. (That's the Hulk version of myself who randomly spirals out about a cup of milk on the counter when the real problem is the division of household chores or a complicated issue at work. She's super fun.) Talking about the thoughts, feelings, and fears that are bouncing around and causing stress turns the internal temperature down inside my brain and helps keep the emotions behind the words from boiling over later. That's a win for everyone.

I haven't always been great at using my words when it comes to my career though and in my experience as a career coach I know this is very common. It comes back to the idea of feeling scared to share because you're putting yourself out there and you're unsure of how others will react. It's also tricky to use your words in the workplace because every company, manager, and industry has different expectations. You need to feel out the situation, weigh the pros and cons, and be tactful in your approach. I fully understand this sounds exhausting and you'd like to go back to talking about the Spice Girls, but we'll make this easier. Promise!

In my case, the manager I eventually opened up to about my big goals of writing, coaching, and having my own business was also a career coach, a mom, and the person who held my hand when I got the test results revealing my third miscarriage in the middle of a work event. This was a person I trusted explicitly and related to deeply, but I still felt nervous talking to her about goals that didn't directly relate to my current job. She didn't even know I had a blog or was writing for big publications until nearly two years after I had been writing nonstop, and how would she know because I didn't tell her. I had bumped up against a passion I didn't fully know was there and it still felt uncomfortable to talk about writing in any professional sort of way. Putting my words out into the world for strangers had become a regular part of my life, but talking about how much I loved doing that with people I knew? And owning up to how much I wanted writing to be a core part of my career? That was awkward and terrifying. Awkifying.

However, I knew I had to get a little brave, sign my own permission slip saying "Becca is hereby allowed to have dreams," and then actually go for it. Otherwise, I was going to slide along in my career continuing to say yes to work I didn't want to do to get to a place I didn't want to go, while saying no to things that brought me great joy.

With that in mind, in the summer of 2018, I sat down with my manager and laid it out there. I loved career coaching, I loved writing, and this work of combining the two for an audience of working moms gave me so much energy that I wanted to do it all the time. I told her that in the early morning and late-night hours I was side hustling to build this business, and even (gasp!) told her about the vision of leaving my current job in two years. I wasn't quitting my job at that moment, and I was still planning on doing all of the technology projects and event planning work in my job description, and doing them very well, but truthfully these things were not what I loved to do. My goals had shifted, and I was going for them.

Sounds like a pretty scary conversation huh? Perhaps a bit risky? Or completely insane? Maybe it was all of those things. But speaking up at that moment was the absolute best thing I could have done for my career because here's how it went down.

My manager listened patiently, asked questions, took notes, and listened some more. Then she did something I wasn't expecting at all by challenging me to think about how I could bring my side hustle passions into my current job while I built my business. Maybe I couldn't write about my childhood crush on Jonathan Taylor Thomas for an audience of MBA students a generation my junior, but perhaps I could write an educational piece that would compare the virtual job search to online dating. Or I could do some digging into unique interview questions or innovative recruiting strategies and make these topics fun to read about. I hadn't even considered the possibility of being more creative at work or getting creative about how I used my creativity. That was silly and stifling.

By using my words, and uh oh, I'm going to type it..."*speaking my truth*" a whole new chapter opened up in my professional life and I started writing really interesting articles for the Harvard Business School recruiter, alumni, and student blogs as part of my day job. Since my manager also now knew I wanted to make more time for career coaching, she supported my efforts to rejigger my schedule as I did more training and developed my coaching expertise and style. The office needed more coaches, especially ones who genuinely loved editing resumes, but I hadn't been raising my hand high enough or my voice loud enough to do it.

After I had that open career development conversation, I felt a boulder lifted off my shoulders. I didn't have to pretend to want to manage a bigger team or climb the ladder. I could embrace who I was and what I wanted while finding ways to do that work in my current job. I want that kind of relief and opportunity for you too! Career stress boulders are heavy and not good for your back, particularly if you aren't getting enough calcium in your diet. Plus it's much easier to push open the next door when you're standing up straight.

Let's take this one slowly though because as I mentioned, every company and every boss is different. I've had coaching clients with managers who supported them through career transitions, and even known some managers who have hired me to help their employees! I've also had coaching clients with The Devil Wears Prada style managers, so needless to say our coaching work was very much under wraps. In your case, you might have a boss who isn't sympathetic to the idea that you are trying to manage a career and manage family, or that you have a vision for "having it all" that doesn't include exactly what you are doing right now. There may be little room for creativity and flexibility in your job because of the nature of the industry. Therefore, the script I used for my manager heart to heart might not be for you, but we can put your spin on it.

To do that, take a pause and think about if your manager

or someone else you trust at your job would be open to having a conversation about your goals. Maybe not a "I hate this job and I'm ready to soar off into the sunset like a majestic eagle!" style rant, but even a toe-dip in the honesty water. Could you talk about wanting to help out on a project that sounds interesting, or could you be honest about your goal to be a manager within the next two years? Could you share with someone at your work more about a passion project you've been working on and how that might relate to your day job? When you approach this conversation be sure that you're doing so in a way that respects the needs of your current employer while also advocating for yourself. Think about what they need from you, think about what you need to be happy. Is there an overlap that you hadn't recognized before? While getting out of that job might be the answer, using your words is one way to love the job you're with when you can't be with the job you love.

Next, think about turning those words you're using into questions. If my kids tell me they like ice cream I might say "Cool, I also like ice cream" and leave it at that. What they were actually doing is covertly asking for ice cream by stating a fact but since they didn't ask, I didn't know to say yes. (I mean, I sort of knew they were asking for ice cream but it was 10 AM and I had already eaten all the ice cream last night so I played dumb.)

The same concept applies to your "use your words" conversation at work. Do you feel like your work isn't being noticed and that's stopping you from getting a promotion? Ask if you could work on a task force that will give you more exposure across the company. Stuck on how to get from point A to point B in your career? Email the Senior VP to request thirty minutes on her calendar to ask her about her career progression. Take a couple of pages from my book, literally and figuratively, and ask to job shadow someone with more experience just like I did when I trained to be a career coach. I asked my manager and several other career coaches if I could watch them coach, and then asked them each a million questions about their style, coaching frameworks, and strategies so I could develop my own. Come in prepared with both pieces of this puzzle - goals and ask - and you'll be in much better shape to keep this ball rolling forward.

Using your words about the big changes you want to make in your career and life should happen outside of the office too. Your partner can't help you fulfill your dreams if they don't know what those dreams are. Your kids won't know why you are up in the early morning hours learning a new skill or practicing interview answers in the mirror if you don't tell them. Your neighbor won't tell you about the cool new job at her sister's company if you a) ignore her at the mailbox or b) don't open up about looking for a new opportunity.

Using your words at work and at home can be scary. Believe me, I understand. We worry about what people are going to think, we worry that we might sound silly, we worry someone's going to take a hammer to our dreams. But the alternative is not doing the thing you really want to do throughout your whole life. Dude...that's way scarier.

———

Some closing thoughts on using your words, courtesy of Jack.

If you are truly using your words with yourself and other people in your life – that's good. You go, Glen Coco! However, it's important that we don't just use our words, but that we use honest words. I like to think of myself as an honest person; we probably all do. That's one of those big virtues that is pretty taboo to rebel against. But are we ever really, really, REALLY honest? Like three-year-old honest?

For my 33rd birthday, Glen organized an adults-only dinner out for us and a small group of friends. We see each other a lot with our kids, but very rarely get to spend time sipping wine in a restaurant without cutting up a child's grilled cheese sandwich into smaller bites because "it's too spicy." I was thrilled to be going out, and for the first time in a while put on some clothes that weren't designed for the office or athleisure. Jack looked at me and said:

"Mommy, why are you wearing that pretty dress?"

"I'm going out to dinner with Daddy."

"But he's not wearing anything special."

Jack clearly delivered a sick burn, and he made an important point. Two actually, because Glen really could have put in a little more effort. The other point, though, is that sometimes beating around the bush is a waste of time. You might need to dial back the full-on honesty for that conversation with your boss slightly. I mean, don't go tell her to change her clothes. But keep being three-year-old honest with yourself and your partner. Don't sugarcoat it, tell the real truth, even the stuff that seems scary or hard. You'll get to the point a lot quicker that way and save yourself some time to binge Season 4 of *Parks & Recreation* on Netflix.

(That's the season when Leslie Knope begins her campaign for City Council and honestly, it's just so good that I need to take a break from writing to go watch it again. See you in a little bit.)

CHAPTER 6 NOTES

Use Your Words

Be honest with yourself.

Are you as happy in your career as you'd like to be? Do you have a big goal that you're afraid to say out loud? Start by writing it down.

Be honest with your partner/friend/family.

Does someone important to you know how you feel about your career? Do they know about a goal you have for yourself? Challenge yourself to tell them.

Be honest at work.

Is there anyone you could talk to at work about your goals (mentor, boss, trusted colleague)? Have you asked about taking on new projects, delegating tasks that are a better fit for someone else, or doing more training? Challenge yourself to have the conversation.

MAKE NEW FRIENDS

"You must be so excited about school!
You're going to meet so many new friends!"
"Oh look, here comes a new friend to the playground!"
"Go ask those kids if you can play too.
Make some new friends!"

*A*s a parent, I've become quite a friend pusher. This is partly because I want to sit quietly on a bench for a few minutes at the playground, but it's mostly because I know how important friendships are to me and I want that for my kids. If Jennifer Aniston taught me nothing else, it's that friends will be there for you when the rain starts to pour so, like many other moms and dads out there, I'm giving my kids a nudge out of my nest at every friend making opportunity. Then, whenever my kids tell me the best part of their day was playing with their friends I pat myself on the back and feel pretty good about my parenting skills for the moment. Until I screw up 15 minutes later and get all ranty about ketchup distribution because parenting is hard.

My child friendship matchmaking doesn't take that much effort though because making new friends comes pretty easily to kids. "You like red? Oh, wow I like red too! Best friends forever!" However, meeting new people as an adult is a lot harder than when you were a kid. For one, you generally need more than a favorite color to build a base of adult friendship. Then there is simply the awkwardness of it all. How can I get another adult to go from being an acquaintance to being my friend? Does my mom call her mom? Should I just hope that we're in the same homeroom next year?

Another reason it's tricker to make adult friends is the lack of organized friend-making activities. You could join a local group that does monthly Mom's Night Outs or an adult softball league, but maybe you don't have the time. Or maybe you're introverted and all of that sounds terrible. Plus, putting yourself out there is scary! Kids don't worry so much if Jimmy doesn't want to play tag, they find another kid to play tag. For adults though, the fear of rejection gets very real.

Here's an example of just how awkward it can be to make new friends as an adult, or at least how awkward Glen and I made it.

When I was pregnant with Jack, we attended a child-birth class at the hospital. There was helpful information, a hospital tour, and some rather uncomfortable knees up breathing exercises in Conference Room A. Beyond learning about the wonders of dilation and pain medication, the highlight of the class for me and Glen was the couple sitting next to us. Karla and Cassidy were around our age, lived in the town next door, and were expecting their first child just days after our baby was due. Neither of us knew the sex of our babies which instantly bonded us into the "I'm Just So

Chill, I Don't Need to Know" club of pre-parenthood, plus they picked up on our movie references and could talk football. I pulled Glen aside at hour six of the seven-hour class and whispered "I want them to be our friends... How do we make them our friends?"

I was 29 at the time and probably should have developed some social skills by this point, but I hadn't made an honest to goodness new friend in years! The idea of suggesting to a person who didn't go to elementary school with me or lived in my freshman college dorm that we become real-life friends was terrifying. However, the unborn child inside me who might also want friends, and the coolness of Karla and Cassidy, inspired me to broaden my social circle so Glen and I came up with a plan well suited to the online dating world in which we met. We would write our email addresses on a piece of paper and slide it over to Karla and Cassidy at the end of the class. Our smooth line was going to be "It was great meeting you guys. If you want to keep in touch since our kids will be the same age, here are our email addresses." It was the simplest line of all time but we agonized over it the full length of the bathroom break.

Fortunately, Karla and Cassidy were interested in our friendship. They accepted our email addresses without hesitation and passed along theirs. Then Glen and I eagerly checked our messages like 90s teens waiting for the AOL Instant Messenger door to open announcing your crush was now available to chat. We didn't even play it cool and put up an emo away message; we responded to their email as soon as possible to solidify the bond. From final days of pregnancy texts to first playdates at three weeks old, to playgrounds, to birthday parties, our little guys remain friends five years after that day in the hospital. Karla and Cassidy are still our friends too and have laughed at this story about how Glen and I plotted our way into their lives.

————

Having kids does tend to make the idea of meeting new adult friends a bit easier. You can establish common ground pretty quickly when your children appear to be the same age and exchanging numbers at the playground is about the kids so it feels less weird. However, I'm still naturally more introverted and prefer the comfort of the friends I've barnacled onto in my youth. Meeting new people takes energy and most of my energy as a new mom was being channeled into cleaning up spit-up, wondering what that smell was, and texting my already existing friends back 48 hours later.

Therefore, by my early 30s I was tired and feeling a bit shy, which is fine, but here's the rub. I was also having all of these life epiphanies about making a career change and while you can try to do that on your own, it doesn't always work out so well. To run my own businesses I needed to talk to people who ran their own businesses to learn how they did it. To get my writing further out there into the world I needed to build relationships with writers and publishers who knew the ropes. To get coaching clients I needed to meet more potential coaching clients. This was all new territory for me after following a straight career line for many years and I had a lot of learning to do. More specifically, I had a lot of networking to do.

Before you run for the hills because I'm about to talk about networking, please stick with me! I get that people hate the word networking, and for a long time, I did too. It feels sleazy, like you are purposefully working to throw a net over people and tie them into your inner circle for your personal benefit. It gets worse when you use the phrase "building your network." Now you are an evil genius plotting to throw the net over people. It's not even happening organically. Gross. Networking is the word we are left with though because "make new friends, and keep the old, one is silver and the other's gold" isn't catching on in the world of business. It's probably too long. So let's use the word networking and try to break free from the negative connotations that I just put in your head.

Start with "net." Let's pretend it's not the kind of net you use to catch a fish or nab bank robbers in a cartoon. Instead, think about the word "net" in networking as a hammock. A cozy hammock that we as parents haven't reclined in for many, many years because kids, but the memory is there. Through strong connections between ropes, a hammock net supports your body weight, lifts you off the ground, and makes sure you don't plummet into the rocks below. Wouldn't you want that kind of net in your life? Not the kind of net that you throw over people, but the kind of net that supports you and provides support to others. Sounds kind of like friendship, right? Because it is. Personal and professional friendship.

Now for the "working" part of networking. Let's get over to HomeGoods and reframe this picture, shall we? What if you weren't trying to work people, but work WITH people? When you think about it, that's what we are all doing every day. As parents we are working with our partners, childcare providers, teachers, and family members to raise our kids well. As professionals, we are working with our colleagues, clients, and business partners to develop strategies, create products, and reach revenue goals. Working with others applies to even the most solo of soloist career paths. Do you want to write a book? Even if you write that book entirely on your own, edit it, cut down the trees to make the paper, and print it out using ink that you squeezed from homegrown blackberries, you are going to need someone else to buy that book if you want to make any money from it. We need other people in this life; we need teammates. That whole "working" part of networking – its team working.

In our less icky version of networking, we're left with a process of strengthening the ropes of our hammocks and building our teams. The people already in your life, your friends and family, are super important parts of your team because they will support you, give you a boost when you need it the most, and offer tough love when you could use a reality check. Your personal network also might be able to introduce you to more people in your career field if you ask! You can do the same for them too. That's how your personal network can merge with your professional network over time.

Then think about your existing professional network. Your current and former coworkers share the hot office gossip and go halfsies on the last glazed donut with you, but they also share important career history with you and will be your references for future job applications. Your current and former clients can provide testimonials and referrals for your work too. Keep up with those professional relationships you've already developed with a note to say hello or grabbing lunch from time to time. It doesn't take much to keep people in the know about what you're up to and ask about what they're up to too. Then you won't feel weird asking someone for a recommendation or introduction down the road because it won't be the first time they've heard from you in years!

Now we get to the "make new friends" part of creating

your team. Building a network you can learn from and grow your career with is going to require meeting new people, and if you're shy or self-conscious then that's not always comfortable. This is especially true of the traditional networking event which looks like sticking on a name tag, walking into a room full of new people, holding a small plate of crackers and cheese, and making small talk about the crackers and cheese with strangers. I don't know about you but I'd rather have my crackers and cheese on the couch with some Netflix.

However, conferences and local networking groups can be amazing ways to meet new people who can support you in your career, so one tip I use to force myself out of my jammies is to work with a networking event buddy. Not only will your buddy provide you some much needed social anxiety comfort at events you attend, but they can also act as your accountability partner. You may not mind letting down 45 strangers at an event, but you will feel a sense of responsibility to your friend if you bail.

My friend Amanda is that person for me. She dragged me kicking and screaming to my first networking event, kicking and sighing to my second networking event, and doing a little jig of excitement going to my third networking event. I've met new clients, collaborators, and friends at these events and all of this has made me realize there's something to be said for cheese, crackers, and new people. If you're feeling brave enough to hit up events on your own, go for it! And if you're a bit more like me, then find a fearless Amanda and let her rub off on you.

You don't need to go to hive-inducing non-jammie-wearing mixers to expand your network though. Instead you can go the online dating route and take your friend-making virtual. For a while, in writing I was going it solo by posting on my blog, submitting articles to other websites unsuccessfully, and wondering how other writers seemed to already know each other. Well, as it turns out, they didn't just happen to be in the same homeroom, the writers I admired knew each other because they put the effort in online.

I finally figured that out when a fellow blogger found my writing entertaining and invited me into a group of mom bloggers connected on Facebook. This little group of funny moms kickstarted my online networking adventure as we shared each other's writing and offered feedback. These women taught me about other ways to grow my writing portfolio, inspired me to submit to new publications, and introduced me to more digital friends. Sure, I have never been face-to-face with any of the women in my writing network, but thanks to the glorious internet age it doesn't matter. We've swapped emails, spoken on the phone, chatted over Zoom. Real-life in-person meetups are cool, but that's not always doable, or particularly appealing to social Nervous Nellies, so this kind of from the couch, shared interest group, one on one networking is an equally effective alternative.

———

"Okay, Becca, this is all well and good but what am I supposed to say to these strangers after I meet them? You didn't exactly give me a great professional friend making script with your awkward passing of notes in childbirth class story," you say, still skeptical about networking. That's a fair critique. Duly noted. Don't worry though, I do have the answer to this question. Ask questions.

We know that kids like to ask questions. A lot of questions. One day when Jack was three and Norah was getting on two, I decided to quantify my slow descent into madness and count how many questions they asked in one day. I made it until 7:00 AM and 105 questions before realizing that I needed to reserve the brainpower I was using for counting for trying to remember why astronauts' suits are white and not red. And why don't skunks wear pants? Also, where is that lollypop Jack got at the parade three months ago? (Under the car seat, unfortunately.)

Kids ask questions because they are naturally curious about the world. In fact, studies have found that human beings are at their most curious around age four[1], which checks out based on my experience living with four-year-olds. However, some adults carry that curiosity around with them for a lot longer and there is so much to learn from those people.

For example, my dad, who has had a successful 35+ year career in sales, taps into his curiosity regularly. When Pop meets potential clients he asks them a lot of questions so that he can understand what their pain points are in their businesses, then with that information he can propose a solution his company can offer. However, he's also asking clients, friends, family members, and strangers questions about their lives and their interests because he genuinely wants to get to know people and has a natural talent for making others feel heard and special.

At the end of a conversation with my dad, people always walk away thinking, "Wow, what a cool guy!" even if he didn't reveal a whole lot about himself. He follows the Dale Carnegie motto "Be interesting by being interested" which means if you want other people to think you are interesting, don't make it all about you, instead be interested in them and ask questions.

We're all a little naturally self-involved and the topic we likely know the most about is ourselves, so by leaning into this and asking people questions about their lives you'll not only learn a lot but you'll also make someone else feel great and leave a lasting impression.

Let's take "be interesting by being interested" into that cheese and crackers networking situation we just talked about to show how this not only works for sales but also for networking. You're at the event eating your crackers and breaking a sweat because I told you to go try one of these things but your networking buddy went to the bathroom and now you're all alone. You take a deep breath, go over to someone who looks friendly and introduce yourself.

Then instead of saying "Some weather we're having lately" you start asking questions. "What do you do? Oh, interesting, how did you get into knitting coats for squirrels? What do you enjoy about the squirrel coat making business? "My kid asked me earlier about skunk pants, is that a thing?"

Suddenly you're talking up a stranger without actually having to say too much because they are on center stage of this conversation. Not so bad right? And if you want to get into the small mammal clothing industry then you've found a great contact, but if not you still learned something and made someone feel heard so that's a win!

Like we've talked about, you don't have to go to that cheese and cracker fest to network and ask questions though. Talk to the other mom at the park about what the biggest challenges are in her industry. Send a message to your old high school friend and ask her how she got into teaching yoga. Ask your friend of a friend who owns her own business how she got started. Find someone who went back to school in her 30s and ask to hop on the phone with her for 20 minutes to see how she made it work with her busy schedule. In each one of these situations, you're communicating to someone else how valuable their advice and experience is, you're learning important nuggets of information for your career, and you're making new connections. That's a whole lot better than staring at someone silently thinking "Please be my friend!" right?

When I've forced my clients to go make some friends over the course of our coaching sessions, they always come back with wins. Alex chatted up an alum from her school and learned how her project management skills could be put to good use in the healthcare industry. Laura talked to a friend of a friend and figured out that a career in higher education would be the perfect match for her interests and goals. Maria talked to local entrepreneurs and learned that she had the experience needed to set up her own consulting business, and she even got advice on how to file the paperwork. Not a single one of them felt like they were throwing the net over people or working people; they were meeting people, asking questions, and having a darn good time with it!

Meeting new people and expanding your network can be uncomfortable and not every meeting or chance encounter is going to be a firework show of new job opportunities, just like every first date doesn't end in marriage. However, when you go in with the question asking mindset the whole process becomes a lot easier. To kick this off for yourself, use the notes page at the end of this chapter to write down ways you could push yourself out of your friend making comfort zone to meet some new people. Maybe it's that yoga class you have been meaning to go to, joining the Facebook group of aspiring florists, or simply saying "Hi,

Sachin's mom from daycare. I'm Becca, what's your actual name?" Then set goals for yourself to do those things you wrote down. You can do this!

————

Making new friends that will help you move your career forward comes down to some very simple principles. One, people are important, so treat people like they are important. Two, if you're curious like a cat when meeting new people everyone wins. (Or maybe be curious like Curious George, because curiosity didn't kill him, but it did turn him into a syndicated success with solid merchandise sales. That's a better example.) Three, be yourself and make friends in your own adorably awkward way; there isn't one right way to do this. And lastly, and most importantly, be kind.

Kindness means stepping out of your comfort zone to reach out when someone looks lonely because you might just make their day. It means treating people with respect and listening to what they have to say. It means caring about others for the sake of caring about them, not simply for our own gain. And kindness also means remembering your manners. No one is jumping up and down to help the person who starts the networking conversation saying "So, here's my resume. Can you get me that job?" just like no one is super excited to provide juice to the preschooler who is demanding juice at the top of her lungs. Once Norah tried that and broke the sound barrier. We are proud of her scientific achievement but we miss our hearing. She also did not get the juice.

However, the person who asks nicely for a few minutes

of sometime else's time, asks questions, listens, and offers to reciprocate favors is going to see a lot more yeses and make lot more friends, just like the preschooler who asks, "May I have a cup of juice please?" is going to see a lot more juice in her life. She even might get a cookie to go with it. See what I'm saying? If you give a mom some courtesy and respect...

CHAPTER 7 NOTES

Building Your Net(work)

Who do you already know?

Your existing network is important. Think about all of the people who already know, like, and trust you. This list will include family, friends, neighbors, coworkers, former coworkers, parents from your children's school, etc.

Who would you like to know?

Would it be helpful if you knew someone who worked at your dream company? How about someone who has gone back to work after some time away? Would you like to be able to chat with someone who has started their own business? If you have specific names, list them out here, but even a list like "Someone who has done XYZ" is great!

How could you meet those people?

Could anyone from your first list help you meet someone on your second list? Before you say "Nope!" have you asked?

Then branch out to think about saying "yes" to that alumni networking event invite you usually ignore, or joining a Facebook group of professionals in your areas of interest, or using LinkedIn. There are options!

FOLLOW THE RULES

*L*ittle kids are great at a lot of things, like making inappropriate comments in public restrooms and getting syrup in their hair. However, what kids are perhaps the best at is doing exactly what they want to do. If playing with trucks is going to make a kid happy, she is going to play with trucks. If a kid is going to get more joy from the giraffe stuffed animal than the walrus stuffed animal, then he is going to choose the giraffe. Kids understand instinctively that they have the power to control their own happiness.

As part of that truly wonderful instinct, kids also develop another trait that is equal parts infuriating and inspiring: questioning the rules. "Why do I need an adult with me when I go to the park? Why can't I bring toys to the table? Why can't we watch a movie right now? Why is it a bad idea to slide down the stairs in the laundry basket?" To be fair, that last one sounds amazing and I've thought about it myself on several occasions. But still, my adult answer needs to be "Because you'll crack your head open, and because I said so!"

Kids are running through their days spitting out one long run-on sentence that eventually ends in why because they just want to go do their thing and rules stand in the way. Questioning the rules and why things are the way they are is how kids make sense of the world around them, and why as parents we can barely keep our eyes open past 8 PM. It's exhausting making the rules, enforcing the rules, and then defending the rules you put in place to ensure your children live to see another tomorrow. Little humans, can we just fall into line here please? These are the rules. They make sense for your health and safety as well as my sanity and they aren't going anywhere.

On the flip side of this, when I was a child I never drove my parents crazy. Not one single time. Ask them and they will tell you I was a perfect angel who never broke or questioned a single rule. My very existence made every single one of their days magical. I was a gosh darn delight.

Except for all of those times when I wasn't because that's not true at all. I never stopped talking as a young kid, was bossy as all get-up, and I questioned everything. I know we're supposed to say "I had leadership skills" but I think I was just bossy. Now as a parent of very curious, precocious, and loud little people, my parents constantly laugh at my exasperation when one or both of them go rogue.

However, my parents also have plenty of stories from when I drove them crazy by turning into a rule-following perfectionist. Into my elementary, middle, and high school years I embraced my firstborn child role and started to like rules because following the rules meant you got praised. Ooo, nice words about me? Yes, please! I became so nerdy about rule-following that I was the 16-year-old who called my mom to pick me up from a party because there was alcohol there. I wasn't even drinking it; I was just uncomfortable with the idea of being in the same zip code as underage drinking. I got so good at following rules that I even spent several of my teenage years as a soccer referee to help enforce them.

Rules offered my ambitious people-pleasing heart an outline for how to reach my goals and find success. Since my goals included good grades, approving adults, and pocket change to buy a toe ring at the mall, following rules worked for me, even if it did make me kind of intense to live with. Quite the switch up for the child who often marched around shirtless in her youth because fabric restricted the true nature of her three-year-old essence.

So now we've landed here with these two competing forces in mind, breaking the rules to find joy and following the rules to achieve your goals. It's because I believe both are true that the rules chapter needs to be neatly split into two: Part One - Following the Rules and Part Two - Breaking the Rules. Embracing a bit of both can help take us places in our lives and our careers.

Part I: Following the Rules

Besides the pure exhaustion of it all, why else does it drive us bananas when our kids don't follow the rules? I think a lot of it is because when kids break the rules we might end up driving to the Emergency Room when we specifically shouted, "We don't jump on Mommy and Daddy's bed. If you fall off and hit your face I'm not driving you to the Emergency Room."

Besides the unwanted ER visits, there is also an undercurrent of feeling disrespected when the rules we set aren't followed. I can't tell you the number of times I've boiled over because Jack and Norah were ignoring me and my rules to do whatever they wanted at the moment. While I respect their individuality, I also expect respect as their mother, and I expect them to respect each other. Listen to each other's words, hands to yourselves, and if someone is already grumpy please don't poke the bear. Respect for one another is the biggest rule of them all around our house.

R.E.S.P.E.C.T. Don't show me some and you'll lose TV. Sock it to, sock it to me, put your socks away for me.

When it comes to your career development, respecting others should also be a rule that stays firmly at the top of the list. Respect a potential employer by showing up on time to an interview, respect your colleagues by putting forth your best effort on projects, and respect that you aren't the only voice in the room so that you can learn and grow. Plus all of that respectful behavior is good professional etiquette, it's effective for reaching your goals, and put simply, it's nice.

Unfortunately, respect in the workplace doesn't always come naturally to people because there is something about career progression that brings out our inner "me, me, me!" While there is evidence that a "me, me, me" mindset does work out for some people, we'll all achieve more if that mindset gets pushed out by smart people like you who care about others. However, let's not get respect confused with turning into a "yes woman" and toeing the company line so that you don't ruffle feathers. You can and should stick up for yourself, share your opinion, and point out issues as you take the reins of your career. Ruffle things up! Just do so in a way that shows you are considering others' time, perspectives, and efforts and expect the same kind of respect back.

Another good rule to follow in your career is any meaningful rule you set for yourself. In his book, *The Perfect Day Formula,* Craig Ballantyne[1] discusses how he achieved career success as an entrepreneur and a big piece of his plan was creating a set of personal rules and sticking to them. He equates the personal rule theory back to being pregnant, which is an analogy that I think you'll be able to sink your teeth into too, even if someone without a uterus talking about pregnancy raises a big old red flag of "nope!" He makes a good point, and I've been pregnant several times to vouch for this.

Think back to when you were pregnant and the rules that you were supposed to follow from your doctor. No drinking, no sushi, no soft cheeses. Thems the rules, so you followed them. You had a little life growing in you who was counting on you to follow the rules for their healthy development so you just did it. What would happen if you kept a list of rules for your life that would help you make progress towards your goals, and you treated those rules with just as much reverence?

One of my big goals was writing this book, and it's a pretty daunting goal. It's so daunting that it would be easy to say, "I don't know where to start, maybe I'll just go make a sandwich and see what's new on YouTube."

Instead of doing that, I pretended that my book was a baby, a growing life if you'll pardon the cheesiness, and made some rules for myself.

1) Set my alarm for 5:00 AM every day.

2) Write something every day.

3) Drink a glass of water right when I wake up.

Each one of these self-imposed rules was directly related to the goal and no one cared about them except for me. Waking up at 5:00 AM gave me an hour of writing time before the kids were awake, most of the time. If I didn't wake up at 5:00 AM then there wouldn't be time to write, simple as that. (We'll talk more about this one in a little bit.) Writing something every day meant that even if my brain felt a little fried, and even if I didn't get my full hour in the morning, I would write something (anything!) down so that I kept momentum. Sometimes those things ended up in this book or on my blog, sometimes they ended up in a Word doc file almost as long as this book that once was called "lines to use elsewhere." It has since been renamed to "deleted lines" and "utter garbage" and then back to "deleted lines" when I felt my confidence needed a boost. The water rule is just to stay hydrated so that I have the energy to manage my long day and don't pass out at the office.

Your rules might look completely different than my rules. My rules might sound horrifying to you. That's the beauty of this theory though: your rules are your rules. No one else's. You make up the rules that mean something to you, and because they mean something to you, you'll stick with them. I think that Norah's rule for herself is to never wear the same pair of pants all day. I'm not thrilled with this rule, but boy does she follow through.

Part II: Breaking the Rules

Following the rules has gotten me far in my life. Credit where credit is due to rules. But at the same time, there have been plenty of rules that have held me back. I bet there are rules that have held you back too. I'm not even talking about career stuff yet, I'm thinking about the early days of motherhood.

Coming home from the hospital with a new baby is beyond frightening. You need to secure your little bundle into the car seat properly, make sure every area of the house is appropriately heated, and know how much this little human should be eating, sleeping, and pooping. It's overwhelming, confusing, and again, thunderbolts and lightning, very very frightening.

You'll hear the joke that parenting doesn't come with a rule book, but that's not true. There are about 14 million rule books that all tell you different things, and that's not even including the stack of pamphlets the nurses hand you along with your tiny baby as they send you on your way. Even as a lifelong nerd, I had homework overload with all of the information. There were so many rules!

What I started to learn, after many tearful phone calls with my mother and the pediatrician's office, was that some of the rules of new parenthood should be held onto tightly and others are perfectly fine to be broken. For example, sleep when the baby sleeps? I think that one must be a joke because if I slept when the baby slept I would never have finished the laundry or learned who won Project Runway that season. Those things were important too. Breastfeed for a year? I walked into motherhood with a bag full of high expectations and lanolin but breastfeeding didn't work out and the kids are fine. No screen time until two years old? Sorry, not sorry, I broke that rule. Tell me what is wrong with 20 minutes of PBS Kids while I empty the dishwasher and burn some chicken. Never mind, don't tell me what's wrong with that because I'm going to do it anyway.

Learning that it was okay, and sometimes healthy, to break the rules was very freeing. Breaking the rules and finding my own way also helped me to chill out when my kids started to break rules that didn't actually matter. For instance, it didn't matter that Jack wore his clothes backward for nearly a year. He was picking out his own clothes and dressing himself, which saved me a solid ten minutes in the morning, and he got to express his independence in a way that didn't involve trying to stir the hot pot of macaroni and cheese. Since Jack liked to wear the clothes backward this also meant that he stuck with sweatpants most days so I didn't have to feel bad about not ironing the forgotten khakis at the bottom of the drawer.

For Norah, she breaks all the "rules" of fashion on the daily. She pairs Jack's old soccer jerseys with brightly colored gym shorts and knee-high socks. She wears football pants with brown boots and bedazzled tank tops. The girl has never chosen a matching outfit once, in her entire life, unless you count the full T-Rex costume that she wore down to breakfast the other day.

I'm not 100% chill about my children's fashion, I'm not that cool. There have been plenty of times I've had to catch myself from falling into the rule-following trap when they walk downstairs in baffling outfits. Their outfits might be baffling to me, but that's because I have a preconceived notion of how they *should* dress and I don't think about how they *could* dress. Those are two very different words and they make a world of difference.

In *Rebel Talent: Why It Pays to Break the Rules at Work and in Life*, Harvard Business School professor Francesca Gino studied restaurant owners, entrepreneurs, magicians, and pilots who have found success by doing things differently. The common theme she found among all of them was that they questioned why things have been done a certain way, and wondered what would happen if we did them differently. These leaders in their fields each consistently swapped out a "What should I do?" with a "What could I do?" and then they went and tried it. "Should" helps you to follow the rule book, but "could" opens a whole new world of possibility.

I know that I focused way too much on the "shoulds" and less on the "coulds" throughout my twenties. I got a degree in marketing so I should build a career in marketing. I should work hard to earn a management position, even if managing a team wasn't what I actually wanted to do. I should be working in an office from 9 AM to 5 PM if I wanted to be successful. What a should storm!

However, when I started focusing on what I wanted to try my best at, what I could share with others, and used my imagination, I started breaking rules like Chuck Norris broke noses! I could bootstrap my businesses without winning the lottery. I could write a book without a degree in Creative Writing or being a famous actress. I could create my own job so that I could work and be home with my kids. These were big rules to break, and like so much of this process, it was scary. Breaking rules? Yikes - what would my high school principal have to say about that? If you know Mr. Kelly please don't tell him. He'll never trust me to do the morning announcements again.

Before breaking any of these big career rules that I had been following, I let my rule-following heart take this one slow. If you and rules are also besties, then try taking some of these baby rule-breaking steps first before you go flying off the handle, marching into work to quit, and dancing around downtown in your skivvies because rules are for the birds. Some of my baby rules that I broke while working up the courage to break the big ones included:

I need to work through lunch otherwise I'm not being productive. After my kids were born there was no more sticking around the office to finish one more thing. At 4 PM it was pencils down, run to the car, and try to move other cars out of the way with the power of wishful thinking so I could get to daycare on time. I felt like I was constantly living like the White Rabbit in Alice and Wonderland. "I'm late, I'm late, I'm late." So it shouldn't be surprising that I didn't think I had time to take a break during the day.

One day I decided to break the "work through lunch" rule by forcing myself away from the desk for a half-hour of mild to moderate exercise around noon. This rule breaking stuck and it led to quick catch up calls with other working mom friends on lunchtime walks, a less drowsy version of myself at 2:30 PM, and a more productive and energized afternoon. A little afternoon exercise break also helped me ditch the guilt about not dragging my tired bones to the elliptical machine at 9:00 PM when my bones did not want to be moving. Breaking one rule led to a new personal rule that works much better.

To be good parents, Glen and I both need to be up early with the kids on the weekend. Man-to-man parental defense is certainly easier than trying to play the zone when one kid is throwing elbows in the lane and the other is slam-dunking their applesauce into the couch. However, as my kids have gotten a little older and start to ease into a weekend morning (Norah) or bound into it (Jack) they only need one adult to get up and turn on some cartoons.

Since instituting a new Becca gets up on Saturday, Glen gets up on Sunday rules to break our existing rule, I get an extra hour of writing in each week while tucked away in my room. Those small pockets of time added up to many chapters and blog posts, and the kids don't even notice I was gone.

To be taken seriously I need to write seriously. This rule was all in my head, and likely a holdover from reading lots of textbooks. However, I didn't take Brene Brown any less seriously when she cracked jokes or told funny stories while teaching about shame and empathy. I didn't disregard Hannah Gadsby and Trevor Noah when they talked about discrimination because they happened to be doing it as part of their stand up routines. Breaking that arbitrary rule of either being funny or being serious, not both, helped me learn to embrace my natural writing style, and eventually write 200+ pages in that natural style. And check you out, you're still reading, still laughing, and still taking me seriously when I pester you to do homework!

Speaking of homework, what rules do you have for your career that are holding you back? In addition to the rules we've already talked about, here are some more rules that I've heard from my coaching clients that might sound familiar.

I went to law school so I should work in a traditional legal career. I need to work hard now so that I can do what I actually like to do when I retire. I need to work outside of the home to be a working mother and show my daughter what she can achieve.

When you push on these rules you'll find that they are pretty flimsy. Rules about what defines success, rules about what constitutes good work, rules about who your paycheck comes from - they are all created in your head based on what you've seen others do. But other people aren't you!

You're going to find a notes page at the end of this chapter that has two sections, one for personal rules and one for rules you want to break. If you want to fill up these sections to the brim, that's cool, but I'm going to suggest starting with just one or two in each. That way when you look at your list it feels doable and you can take some action to both make and break the rules. When you're ready to build on your list, come on back to this chapter and add more rules that will keep you moving onward, upward, sideways, or whichever way you want to go!

And since you're coming back anyway can you grab some White Out? Pretty sure there is a typo on page 176 so if you could be a dear and get rid of that extra comma it would be much appreciated.

Rules provide a beautiful dynamic tension as we live our lives as parents and professionals. We need to hold tight to some rules to provide structure and order, and at the same time, we need to let go of other rules that are holding us and our children back. We need to find the balance between total control and total chaos so the wheels don't come off the party bus.

When Glen and I say "Don't wake up Mommy and Daddy at 1 AM to ask if we are going to have dessert tomorrow" that's a good rule. But when we say "Don't wear underwear over your pants," it feels kind of unnecessary. Why is that a rule? The kids aren't hurting anyone with their unconventional fashion choices. When I teach my kids "We always say please and thank you" that is a good rule, but when I try to lay down the law on "Don't go outside when it's raining," the rule doesn't hold much water. Pardon the pun. Why can't the kids go out in the rain, Becca? They might melt? They might get water on the floors that could honestly use a good mopping anyway?

Fortunately in the summer of 2018, I had recently read Francesco Gino's words in *Rebel Talent* and was feeling a bit rebellious myself. Let's go break some rules! So, as Jack and Norah loitered by the back door after a full day cooped up inside, I thought about my rule. Would the kids really get a cold if they played outside for a little bit? No, probably not. Was it that big of a deal if their clothes got wet? No, they were already covered in ketchup from dinner and a little pre-rinse might help actually.

With that, I let loose, opened up the door, and two toddlers sprinted past me running in drippy circles all around the deck. From the dry refuge of the dining room I watched them giggle together for a few minutes, but then realized I didn't need to stay inside when it rained either. I wasn't getting graded on how dry I was going to stay that night, but my kids might very well remember the night they danced in the rain with Mommy.

As I felt the rain on my skin it was like being transported back to the earliest days of my childhood, running wild and free without a care in the world. Glen joined us out on the deck and the four of us caught raindrops on our tongues and "flew to the clouds" with the adults lifting the small humans up to the down pouring sky. We tickled, belly laughed, and danced around with reckless abandon. I mean not entirely reckless, we still don't stand on the deck railing. That's a good rule. But the silly rule, the stifling rule, the rule that was holding us back, that rule was gone and replaced by a new personal rule. When in doubt, choose joy.

I'll remember that day for a long time, and I hope they do too. Jack even brought it up over dinner the other night, a whole year later. Man, we would have missed out on a lot if had followed the rules.

CHAPTER 8 NOTES

Rules to Set For Yourself

What rules can you set to help you reach your goals? Examples: "I wake up a half-hour before the kids during the week." "I reach out to one new person each week to expand my network." "I set aside 15 minutes each morning to write out my top three goals for the day."

Rules to Break

What rules do you have now that you can break? Examples: "To be successful, I need to work 60 hours a week." "I went to college for XYZ major, so that's what I need to do my whole career." "My job isn't in a creative industry, so I can't be creative."

PART III

FOR WHEN THE GOING GETS TOUGH

Building your fulfilling career isn't always sunshine and rainbows. Let's talk about that.

LIFE'S NOT FAIR

"That's not fair!" Jack yelled at me as I explained the punishment for copping an attitude one too many times and then slamming a door in my face.

"There are consequences for your behavior," I replied, feeling proud of my ability to stay calm, "so you have lost TV time for the week."

Of course, I immediately regretted this decision because TV is about the only activity that produces quiet time around these parts, but I had to stay strong. "And that means you don't get to use your Kindle either"

That did it. "Noooooo. No fair!" Jacked cried out as if I had taken away all of the love, happiness, and sugar-based cereal in North America and then he stormed off to his room.

"Life's not fair," I muttered under my breath while slowly counting to four like Daniel Tiger's mom taught me.

Was it a fair punishment? Absolutely. More than fair. Our family had just spent a week at the beach for vacation and after we got home we picked up the new puppy I had finally broken down and agreed to. Jack and Norah loved their new dog, Diggie, and they had just eaten ice cream, swam in the ocean, and stayed up late for seven days straight. Their life was pretty darn amazing at the moment and I wasn't in any mood to listen to grievances. Plus screens are Jack's Achilles heel and maybe if I took them away he would remember that he didn't need to fall apart when things didn't go his way.

In the back of my mind though I knew exactly what the problem was - me and Glen. To make vacation magical during a year that had thus far been less than magical, we had been very lax on the rules and given into requests one too many times. It was like that scene in Willy Wonka and the Chocolate Factory when Veruca Salt falls down the garbage chute and the Oompa Loompa's chastise Mr. Salt for spoiling his kid. "You know exactly who's to blame. The mother and the father." I did not want to be a Mr. Salt. If that meant doling out some more punishments, sometimes punishments that impacted us too and make our house louder and let us sit down less, so be it. Ugh, parenting is hard. So unfair...

Putting things into perspective, a perspective that 5-year-olds don't have yet, the TV issue is not that big of a deal. Jack was right that life isn't fair, but it's not fair in much bigger ways. There are diseases, disasters, hardships, racism, sexism, ableism, hatred, and inequality. There are mean spirited people, pathological liars, people who put others down to lift themselves up, and haters who are going to hate. It would be nice to shield our kids from these hard truths, and maybe we can for a little while, but there comes a point when it's our responsibility to teach them about what really isn't fair and how to deal with it or fight against it. If we don't teach our kids about the unfairness of life, someone else will and it will likely not come packaged in a hug of understanding and support.

There are also times when we simply don't have a choice about whether or not we are going to teach our kids about how unfair life is because they can see it with their own eyes and feel it in their hearts. It's in those times we need to find our adult coping mechanisms to manage our feelings of unfairness to help the kids manage theirs.

For example, remember how I mentioned the year we got Diggie was a not so magical year? It was 2020. Yes, THAT 2020. To put it lightly, it was a no-good very bad unfair year.

————

As a reminder if you're reading this while kicking back in your flying car ten years from now, here's a quick recap of some of the terrible things that happened in 2020.

Australian wildfires took over the continent. A pandemic swept the globe and a virus called COVID-19 killed hundreds of thousands of people. A massive recession occurred because businesses had to shut their doors to stop the spread of disease. The US continued to battle racial injustice, violence, and police brutality. Schools shut down and teachers had to learn to engage kindergartners on a computer while parents had to learn how to homeschool 5th-grade math. Working parents didn't sleep for several months on end without childcare. Ruth Bader Ginsburg died. There were UFO sightings and basically no one cared. Oh and murder hornets sprang up out of nowhere. Does anyone even really remember the murder hornets?

Through all of this disaster, income inequality was glaring, the gender wage gap was glaring, issues with the division of household labor and childcare responsibilities were glaring, and everyone was glaring at each other to make sure we stood six feet apart... There was a lot of glaring. Or maybe it was just people making regular resting faces but it looked like glaring because no one could see your mouth behind the face mask you brought from a woman on Etsy who in 2020 had to abruptly change her business model from selling quilts to selling protective gear. For the majority of the year, we all walked around bathed in hand sanitizer at peak level stress wondering how in the world we were stressed out before all of this went down. Fun, right?

I rode out the pandemic with Glen, Jack, Norah, a houseplant I was bound and determined to keep alive because I have control issues, and eventually Diggie the dog. Our state of Massachusetts was a hotbed of COVID in the early stages of the pandemic so things were shut down and they were shut down hard. Entertainment consisted of too much television, bike rides in the local cemetery because that's not creepy at all, and eating a lot of bread. Until we opened up our little isolation bubble to include my parents an hour away, we did not have any help with childcare, and Glen and I were both working full-time.

As a result, I cried a lot. There are only so many jokes you can make about your kid showing up on your work video conference call before the stress of trying to be all the things to all the people gets to be too much. If you also had young children during the pandemic of 2020, then you completely understand this.

To make matters more stressful and confusing and tantrum-level unfair, Jack was due to start kindergarten in the fall of 2020. Schools had shut down in March to stop the spread of COVID-19 and learning had gone remote through the end of the school year. Jack's wonderful preschool teacher attempted some remote learning with the kids but getting a preschooler to sit still on a Zoom call was, well, let's just say I would rather have been getting a root canal. The idea of Jack starting kindergarten like that, this huge milestone year and the kickoff to his formal education, made me want to throw up in my mouth a little.

Throughout the summer we closely watched the numbers of COVID-19 cases in our district, learned about industry standards for building ventilation, attended virtual school committee meetings and online open houses, and panicked a lot. The options for kindergarten were remote school, in-person school, hybrid confusing model school, every third Tuesday robot school, and find a family of friendly wolves to teach the children survival skills, so it was a real toss-up. Our town decided on a hybrid model, but there was a high likelihood that there would be another surge in COVID-19, another lockdown, and the wolf school I joked about wouldn't seem all that unappealing.

In between pouring my trusty comfort chocolate chips directly into my mouth and filling out school surveys, 2020 also left me looking at my neatly laid out business plans for the year and realizing that I, unfortunately, did not account for a pandemic. Income streams I counted on dried up, safety nets that were stretched out below my big jump to working for myself had some big old holes in them, and I did not know if I was making the right call. Everything about my full-time job screamed "security during a massive recession" and everything about my business screamed, "This may or may not work out. Godspeed."

There were days I handled the uncertainty and indecision like an adult and some days that I crumbled into a ball like a small child throwing an "it's not fair" tantrum. I had worked incredibly hard to get my writing and coaching business to where it was, so the idea of losing the business because staying in my full-time job was the safer choice and there was no longer any time to keep it afloat was devastating for so many reasons. I felt like I would be giving up on myself, I felt like I would be viewed as a failure, I felt like I was scoffing at my own advice to find more fulfillment and joy in your work.

Like many women around the world, I was also looking at the income my husband and I each brought into our family and realizing that if someone needed to homeschool the kids it would likely be me. In our case, Glen and I have different natural talents and interests and those natural talents and interests led us into different fields with different pay scales. Engineering for him, higher education, writing, and coaching for me. I never felt pushed out of the engineering path Glen took because of my gender; I was fortunate enough to be encouraged to go down that path but I didn't want to because I preferred words to numbers.

However, lots of young girls don't get this encouragement to pursue STEM fields that offer higher paying salaries, and the pay disparity later in life reflects this. Girls are also often steered away from leadership roles because being in charge isn't "ladylike" or "nice" and one look at the list of top executives in the United States will tell you girls have heard that message loud and clear. It's getting better, but we're nowhere near equality yet. Taking all of this into consideration, working mothers were the ones taking a career hit, one that may take years to recover from. Talk about unfair.

Through all of these concerns about how the economic fall and pandemic of 2020 was going to impact working mothers on the whole and my own personal career, I also worried if I even trusted my own judgment anymore. I didn't see 2020 coming, what else won't I see coming as I ventured out on my own? Would this new world of increased flexibility and decreased stability be the right call for my family? What if 2020 was the lead up to something more terrible and the worst was yet to come? It was scary, it was unsettling, it was sad, and it felt really, really unfair.

———

I just laid a lot of emotional baggage at your feet with that one, but you are a very good listener so it was easy to do. Also, if I wasn't real with you about 2020 you would understandably think I was a big old liar or had moved off the planet for a year. Plus this is just one real-life example of how the whole idea of parenting yourself to a more fulfilling career is not all peaches and cream and self-assessment. It is hard, confusing, stressful, and filled with roadblocks. It is planning, then adjusting that plan, then crumpling that plan up, tossing it in the trash, and typing up a new plan.

That doesn't mean it's not worth it though. Your success is worth wading through the challenges. Your happiness is worth scaling Unfair Mountain. Your family is worth holding your ground when the world throws a temper tantrum. You're worth it. (Winks at you from a L'Oreal commercial. The very unofficial sponsor of this book.)

As all of the thoughts and fears of 2020 swirled, I took a deep breath, and then I took the advice I always give my coaching clients: when faced with a choice, go back and read your career and life criteria. When I read my list of things that matter most to me, I remembered that what I wanted was time for relationships, the ability to use my creativity, an opportunity to help others, and the thrill of setting and chasing new goals. There was nothing about 2020 that was stopping me from doing the things that made me happiest, in fact, there was an immense amount of opportunity in 2020 to do exactly those things.

If you'll let me dust off my marketing degree for a moment and do a SWOT analysis for 2020 (strengths, weaknesses, opportunities, and threats), the weaknesses and threats of the year were quite clear; there wasn't enough Lysol in the world to clean up those weaknesses and threats. Nor was there any on the shelves. However, 2020 did have its strengths if I looked hard enough and there were opportunities if I was brave enough to take them on.

2020 brought with it slower mornings, inspiring moments with my family, and the opportunity to wear leggings all the time like I wanted to. In 2020 there were many people out there looking for new jobs who started messaging me for help. There were lots of parents who wanted and needed more flexibility in their careers and sought out my advice on how to think about this with their current employers or in something new.

Maybe I had to slow down on some projects, speed up on others, and come up with some entirely new ideas to keep revenue coming in during a recession, but creating new things was why I got into this in the first place. Maybe I had to adjust my plans a bit and hang onto my full-time job for a little longer until there was some clarity on school and childcare, but that wasn't a forever decision. Like everything in this world, it was temporary, and two months after the exit date I had meticulously planned for years had passed I did turn in that resignation letter. The butterflies in my stomach were having a rave as I pressed send, but I did it and forced myself not to look back.

Would it have been more "fair" if everything had gone according to plan and I could have left my job feeling 110% confident that school would stay open, my books would sell like hotcakes, and my client contracts wouldn't fall through? Absolutely. But life's not fair, stuff happens. That doesn't mean we curl up in the fetal position and wait for the asteroid. Scientists think that big one is probably going to miss us by hundreds of thousands of miles. Probably. In the meantime, we had better get creative, play the hands we are dealt, be flexible, contingency plan for the worst, but hope for and expect the best.

Take a minute now and go back to your career and life criteria from chapter three as a reminder of what you said was most important to you. If you're reading this in a time of your life when everything is feeling very unfair and you're forced into making decisions you don't want to make, reflecting on your criteria can give you a helpful perspective.

What is number one on the list? Can you control that? How about number two, three, or four? Find what you have control over that is important to you and focus on that when taking action. Your career and life are not going to look perfect. Nothing is perfect, except for Reese Witherspoon's hair in Legally Blonde and Whitney Houston singing "I Will Always Love You," obviously. Less than perfect can still be pretty darn good though, especially when we approach it with an attitude of treating the rough time as temporary and the potential for better as extraordinary.

————

2020 was a doozy for just about everyone around the world, but many were managing through unfair circumstances I can't speak to from experience. I have lived my life in a place of privilege as a white, cisgender, non-disabled, heterosexual person who grew up in a safe, secure, and economically stable household. While I've worked incredibly hard to get my degrees, earn jobs, build a business, and write books, I've done it while standing on step stools I did not build. These are parts of me I was born into, and in a society that gives you a leg up or pushes you down based on the color of your skin, who you love, and how you identify, those things gave me an unfair advantage.

Some of my coaching clients have similar backgrounds to mine and are approaching career changes with their unique challenges, but with fewer systemic inequities than others. I also have clients who look different than me and top of mind in their job search is finding an organization that won't discriminate against them in hiring or when it comes time for promotions. There are others who are leaving workplaces where they don't feel comfortable speaking up or being their authentic selves. There are clients whose income goals are not simply about them and their immediate families, they are about supporting extended family members managing difficult circumstances after years of being shut out from opportunity.

Some of those same clients are facing the gender wage gap, others are up against a racial wage gap, and others are fighting against both. That disparity adds up to years of lower wages, decreased access to childcare needed for career growth, and significantly less savings and passed down wealth over a lifetime.

All of these factors make career development more diffi- cult. There are more roadblocks, more negotiations, and more considerations and I wish it wasn't like this. I would have loved to have written a book called "Career Develop- ment in a World Where Everything's Fair and Equal!" but I can't write that book right now. Maybe someone else will in the future and I will happily read it and stand in line for a signed copy. Until then I'll do my part to call out the unfairness we're up against in society and admit to my personal step stools. I'll talk to my kids about racism, sexism, ableism, bias, and discrimination, and examine where I've personally missed the mark.

2020 brought a lot of issues to the forefront of my consciousness that I hadn't spent much time thinking about before, and that's on me. As a mother and a career coach, I knew representation was important so kids could see themselves in the professions they admired, but I hadn't fully understood the systemic issues that have held people back from those goals. Thanks to authors like Ijeoma Oluo, Ibram X. Kendi, and Austin Channing Brown who share their lived experience and scholarly expertise, I know more now and can do better so that I'm not just one of the lucky ones on a step stool. Instead, I can contribute to the work of building more step stools that bring us all closer to success.

Part of that is arming all my coaching clients with questions that can help them assess if an organization wants to build more step stools or not.

Does the organization you're interviewing with have staff, with authority and a budget, to dedicate to Diversity, Inclusion, and Belonging? Are there Employee Resource Groups that offer staff places to come together based on race, sexual orientation, or shared lived experience? How does the organization engage with the community? What does staff composition look like across the organization and in leadership roles?

When we all ask these questions eventually it will become impossible for organizations to ignore them. When we all demand that organizations be better, do better, want better then we are part of creating a workforce that offers opportunities for all and not just a select few. When we confront our own biases, make inclusion a priority in our offices, and hire, support, and promote without leaning towards people who look and think like us, we do our part in dismantling unfairness. In doing all of this we make the workforce better and safer for our children. I want that more than anything and I'm willing to bet my bottom dollar that you do too.

I am not an expert on diversity, equity, and inclusion. Not even close. The authors I mentioned above and many other scholars, writers, filmmakers, and speakers out there can speak to this topic with much more detail and nuance than I can. Therefore, the homework part of this section is not me pointing you to a worksheet or asking you to write down your goals. It's about pointing you to places outside of these pages.

Check out Ijeoma Oluo's book *So You Want to Talk About Race?*[1] and Ava Duvernay's film *13*, and the podcast *Code Switch*. Engage in the art of Danika Manso-Brown and dive into the history of racism in the United States and the beauty of multiculturalism. And if you are well-versed and well-educated on the subject of race and inequality and are out there doing the work to dismantle the "isms" that hold us back, thank you. Thank you from the bottom of my heart. There are more of us joining you.

———

As I write this, we are still sitting in the middle of the unfair cluster that was 2020 and I'm crossing my fingers that the giant asteroid I mentioned earlier doesn't rock the planet before I type this next period. (Honestly, I was nervous about tempting fate with that one, but looks like we're good.)

Until there is a widely adopted vaccine for COVID-19

and perhaps for a while after that, we are looking at a long road of uncertainty and stress. Until the economy bounces back, families are going to be struggling. Until women are respected as equals in the workplace and in the home and little girls are encouraged to lead and succeed the same way little boys are, the gender wage gap will continue. Until racism is dismantled at a systematic level with reforms to the justice systems, education, healthcare, and social services, the deep levels of unfairness in the United States will continue.

A lot is going down right now and to put things lightly, our societal "to do" list is quite long. I do believe we'll get there though, and I also imagine that future paleontologists will be examining our teeth in 400 years saying "Hey Janet, why do you think their teeth were ground down to the gums? Must have been stressful back then... Want to go fly around on our Artificially Intelligent unicorns later?"

However, the reason I am so sure we're going to get to where we need to be is these kids. The children you and I are raising are strong, resilient, and kind. They are technological natives who will take their love of screen time and give us inventions we couldn't even have fathomed. They are the budding scientific minds making potions in the bathtub for hours on end because for a while there in 2020 we couldn't leave the house, and they will bring us healthcare advancements that will cure disease. They are the kids standing out in the 100-degree heat wearing masks and holding protest signs. They are the kids, like my Jack, who turn to the adults and say "But why don't adults treat everyone fairly. They are adults, they should know that already."

You're right buddy, we absolutely should know that already. And while I can't promise him that life will always be fair, I can promise him that as adults we will do better. We will learn from our own mistakes and teach these kids how to cope with the unfairness of life by standing up for what is right, using our voices for good, setting boundaries for ourselves and our kids, and being flexible and resourceful when things get hard. If 2020 reminded us of how important these things are then there's the glimmer of a silver lining of this cloudy with a chance of locusts kind of a year.

Ready to do some more hard things? No? Want to take a nap first? Okay, that's cool. But then let's come back and tackle them together. You've got this.

CHAPTER 9 NOTES

What accomplishment are you proud of from 2020?

Write it down. Own it! You managed through a lot as a mother and professional and deserve some serious kudos.

Diversity Inclusion and Equity Questions to Ask of Your Current Employer or Potential Employer

• Does the organization have staff, with authority and a budget, to dedicate to Diversity, Inclusion, and Belonging?

• Are there Employee Resource Groups that offer staff places to come together based on race, sexual orientation, or shared lived experience?

• How does the organization engage with the community?

• What does staff composition look like across the organization and in leadership roles?

OWN YOUR CHOICES

*M*ornings don't always go smoothly around our house. If everyone gets a good night's sleep, has decided to be easy going about spoon color, and can find the specific pair of orange shorts they want to wear then we are good. But, as any parent can tell you, a "good" night's sleep is only being woken up twice, the blue spoon that changes color in the milk actually does make breakfast more fun, and the specific pair of orange shorts is usually in the wash.

One particular morning when Norah was one year old, a lack of sleep caught up to me and I was not at my best. To be fair, she wasn't at her best either though because apparently my rules, the lack of yogurt, and the angle of the sun were all wrong and life-ruining. In a fit of despair and defiance, my dear sweet toddler looked me in the eye, picked up her cereal bowl, dumped the cereal all over the floor, and then proceeded to cry about the fact that she no longer had cereal. Lacking any remaining patience and specific toddler parenting training, I looked her back in her one-year-old eyes and said "Own your choices" and then I walked away.

It was a little harsh. "Own her choices?" Lady...she's a one-year-old, she doesn't own anything except the blonde curls on her little head. But even in my not very empathetic overtired state, I did do a couple of things right in this situation. One, I chose to walk away instead of screaming out of frustration. You've got to know when to hold 'em, know when to fold 'em in parenting, and sometimes walking away is 100% the best option. Two, "own your choices" is not a bad lesson to learn young. The concept boils down to this: if you make a choice to do or not do something, recognize that you were the one to make that choice and then deal with the consequences. For example, dump your cereal on the floor and now you no longer have cereal and that's your problem, no one else's.

Throughout my childhood, this lesson was reiterated every time I failed to help out around the house or didn't put forth my best effort. (It also came up when I knocked out my brother's front tooth while playing rollerblade tag.) There was a direct line between effort and result, choice and consequence, hitting and spending the better part of an afternoon searching through wood chips for a tooth... It's your mess, you clean it up. It's your problem, you fix it. Or perhaps my favorite way of putting this courtesy of my dad's growing list of catchphrases "You bring it, you sling it."

———

Owning your choices falls squarely into the "When the Going Gets Tough" section of this book because this is not an easy thing. There are choices made for us in this life that we need to deal with or fight back against. There are choices we make that are a result of being faced with two equally bad options. There are also choices we make that are, put simply, mistakes and we need to own up to them and learn from them.

We give a customer the wrong order, we type the wrong number in the spreadsheet, or we jump to conclusions instead of checking the facts. We don't try our best, we cheat to win, or we give up on ourselves completely. Or, as a pure hypothetical, we knock out our brother's tooth and then help our mother dip one of our old baby teeth that she kept in a drawer into a bloody towel and then "find" that tooth in the wood chips for our distraught brother. Oh, sorry. Was that disgusting story not universal? Sometimes we tell inappropriate stories in the middle of our books and challenge readers' gag reflexes... Mistakes, big ones and small ones, happen.

I'm not proud of my mistakes, or the blood on my hands, but we all make them. Every single one of us, often several times a day. It's 2 PM and I can think of at least five mistakes I've made since opening my eyes this morning.

As a mother, I have made many more mistakes than I can count as I try to figure out how to parent two very different children. I shouldn't have been so adamant about breastfeeding Jack when it wasn't working. I shouldn't have let Norah walk down the stairs by herself that one time. I shouldn't have yelled. I should have gotten more sleep. I shouldn't have let them listen to "Baby Got Back."

In my work, I have deleted large files by accident, pushed people too hard when they weren't ready, sent the wrong link, undervalued my worth, and failed to check my math. Rewinding my life a bit farther, I recall a very memorable mistake I made as a camp counselor when I forgot to sign up to lead an afternoon recreation event and got assigned to "Fetch with Becca." And yes, the game I had to play with a bunch of preteens at camp that day was literally fetch. They took a big bucket of tennis balls out to a field and I ran to go get them in 90-degree heat. This was 17 years ago and I'm still eating brownies that I claim to have sweated off the calories for that day.

In each of these examples, I made a choice and that specific choice led to a mistake. Not a life-altering mistake (don't worry, it was just a baby tooth), but a mistake all the same. The most important part though is that in each one of these instances I admitted to myself and to others that I made a mistake which in turn allowed me to learn and grow. I never forgot to sign up for an afternoon recreation event at camp again. I double and triple check my emails before sending them. I listen more carefully, think more deeply, and whenever possible I find someone else to do the math. The success that came from making those better choices came from owning earlier choices that weren't so great.

Let's hear from someone else who has made a mistake before you start worrying that I make too many and I'm giving you terrible advice. How about the people who brought you Woody, Buzz, Wall-E, and Elastigirl? There's a story that Ed Catmull tells in *Creativity, Inc.* about the time at Pixar when two years of work on *Toy Story 2* got deleted from their systems. It was a result of a few different mistakes - delete codes that were too easy to type, backup systems that didn't work, and a failure to back up the backup systems.

Fortunately in this situation, a Pixar employee had a backup of the movie on her personal computer because she just had a baby and was doing work from home. Moms get stuff done, y'all. I could end the story there on a "new mother saves Pixar and yes that makes perfect sense" note, but the story is also about mistakes. In this situation and in other situations that followed, Pixar admitted their mistake as a company, owned the choices they had made and didn't point fingers at others, and then built in better security and backup systems so this kind of disaster wouldn't happen again. It hasn't. Mistakes are valuable!

This all seems obvious, right? Take responsibility for your actions, learn from your mistakes, and move on. Yet the reason "Own Your Choices" is a hard lesson to internalize is that we get caught up in the idea that as adults of a certain age we should have it figured out by now, particularly once we become parents and experienced professionals. We give our kids a pass when they forget their lunch at home or knock over the syrup bottle by accident. Mistakes happen, and these are little mistakes. Totally fixable! But for us? No, there's no more time to make big mistakes now, big mistakes are for youths! We have people to raise and car bills to pay! This isn't a coast-through situation, we should be bringing our A-game into working parenthood because we've entered the life or death arena. Armor up, don't screw up.

But while all of that is true and we don't want to mess up, it's also important that we accept that mistakes, big and small, are not just for the youths, they are for everyone. Birthing and raising people doesn't make us any less human, and like other humans, we learn more from our mistakes than our successes. When everyone is clapping for us, our brains are in celebration mode and we don't instinctively think about what we could have done better or differently. When we're following along with the status quo and not trying anything that could lead to a mistake, the silence makes us complacent. However, when a mistake happens and we admit that it's a mistake, we see the consequences first hand, sometimes painfully, and that tiny little stenographer in our brains starts typing. Remember this, don't do that, learn from this. That memo gets delivered up the chain to your brain's senior leadership so they're aware of what went down and can start strategizing how to improve.

Examples of big "mistakes" we try to avoid making in our careers are picking the wrong job, taking a risk that doesn't pan out, or choosing the wrong career path altogether and finding out eight years in that you hate it. These mistakes happen though, frequently in fact, and when they do we have two choices, ignore them or own them. When we ignore them because we're worried about being judged for admitting that we, the grown-up people with good heads on our shoulders, got it wrong, we put a bigger value on other's opinions than our happiness. If you play this out with examples I promise it's going to sound bananas.

Do I care more about my co-worker Nancy's opinion about changing my career path than I do about my well-being as a human? You and Nancy might like each other but you are very different people with different interests and goals. You don't have to stay in a job because good ole Nan thinks leaving your job in accounting to go back to school and be a nurse is weird. Is Nancy going to be funding your retirement, or teaching your kids about following their dreams, or resting her head on your pillow at night? I'm guessing not, so as Joey Tribbiani once so thoughtfully stated in *Friends* Season 7, Episode 8, in this situation Nancy's opinion is like a cow's opinion. Moo.

Should I be so worried that Jerome and Jessica will tsk tsk me over dinner because my startup idea didn't work out? Are their opinions more important to me than my dreams? Jerome and Jessica are lovely people, but they are not you. They are also not big risk-takers and that is 110% fine. We need the Risky Roxannes in life just as much as we need the Steady Susans, and there will be times when you switch up roles in your own life depending on the circumstance.

I was a Susan for years before Roxanning it and taking the leap to focus full-time on my own business. Even though it was a calculated thought out for years risk, I'm sure I was tsked behind closed doors for choosing to leave a very secure job for a decidedly unstable path forward. And the verdict is still out! I could end up back as a full-time employee for another company or University in the future, I don't know for sure.

I do know that disapproving tsks don't have much at all to do with you or me. Jerome and Jessica want us to be happy and successful, and when a risk sounds too big or it doesn't pan out, their tsking is coming from a place of "That choice sounded scary and my bias against risk has been confirmed." That's fine though, own your own choice, not theirs. You didn't bring their choice, you don't have to sling it.

———

When we own our choices and admit the mistakes, the power is in our hands again. We've owned the choice, and now we can learn, grow, and move forward in the direction we want to take our lives. So what are we going to do now that we've owned our choices and want to start taking some action?

Let's start with this example: You aren't totally happy with your job. There are things you can appreciate about it but on the whole, there is well, a hole, and signing up for this job or choosing to stay in this job might feel like a big mistake. If this is you, you aren't alone in this feeling, at all. According to a Gallup poll in 2017, 70% of American workers are disengaged at work.[1] That's a lot of people looking around their cubicle or store or construction site feeling regret over the choices they made.

The easy way out of that feeling is to let the disengagement get to you while you come up with a million reasons why your job sucks. To be fair, it might suck. Your current job could be entirely the wrong fit and the self-reflection you've done so far while reading this book has helped bring that to further clarity. Sorry about that. But jobs, both paid and unpaid, are important and you need to do them. So it's time to use the power in your hands to own your choices and make the most of them. Find some way to make your current job more interesting for your own sake, so that even if you're not in your dream job, you're learning, growing, and making moves towards a change in the future.

For me as a camp counselor playing fetch, the prospect of eating brownies forever and not feeling bad about it was what kept me engaged, as well as giving the kids a memorable afternoon full of side-splitting laughter. For you, it could be giving yourself a challenge to complete a project more efficiently or learn a new skill from a colleague. Making spreadsheets in Excel is not my steaming hot cup of tea but when it was a large part of my job, I learned new formulas from my co-workers that made my projects go by much quicker. Those efficiencies helped give me back more time in my day for writing and taught me to manage the numbers side of my own business.

You could also think about what you have learned from your mistakes and how that is going to help you improve in the future. One of my coaching clients was concerned she made a mistake by becoming a teacher, but then she reframed the teaching job she no longer enjoyed as a chance to hone her presentation skills for a future job as an entrepreneur.

Another client felt like he had made a mistake by jumping on a job offer that sounded appealing before really taking the time to evaluate if it was what he wanted. He and I worked together to think about what he learned from the experience, how he could make the most of the job he had by meeting new people in the industry, and how this experience is going to make him much more prepared to find a future role that does a better job of checking off his career and life criteria boxes.

Sitting back and worrying about how the choices you have made won't get you very far, like the old saying about worrying and sitting in rocking chairs. When you own the choices you've made though, you can get your buns out of the worrying rocking chair, kick the chair over, go pick it back up because the kicking was dramatic but not necessary, and then go do something about the choices you've made and make some better ones.

———

We've been talking a lot about mistakes, but I'd like us to end on a high note and talk about all the amazing choices you've made so far in life. In coaching, I like to focus on strengths more than weaknesses, and I do my best to do that in parenthood too. It's way harder to do in parenthood because I don't really want to give my child credit for her strength in negotiation when we are staring across the table from each other at a plate of asparagus. In that situation, I want to double down on weaknesses and explain precisely how her refusal to eat two bites of this small green vegetable is negatively impacting my life. However, when possible, I help my kids lean into their strengths, encourage their interests, and give them positive feedback to both boost their confidence and help them see that we recognize their good behavior and best efforts. That positive reinforcement goes a long way for kids, and it's helpful for adults too.

One big incredible choice you've made - motherhood. You made a choice to bring children into your life and raise them to be kind people who work hard. The world needs those types of people to keep our society moving forward, what an amazing choice motherhood is! Plus while there are times when motherhood can completely knock you out, it's also wonderful and it's part of your soul at this point. I know it is for me.

I wear a lot of hats in my career, community, and family, but my motherhood hat is the one on there most securely, like a swim cap that's held on even more firmly in place by the one million bobby pins required for a prom up-do. Wearing this hat is a choice I made, and I wouldn't change it for the world. I don't think you would either.

When I look around the internet and listen to you on the playground, I also see you choosing to admit that motherhood can be challenging and I can't applaud you louder for that choice! In a lot of ways, I think this admission that it's hard makes motherhood easier. It's a bit of a paradox but it's true. When you can both own the choice you made to be a mother and own the fact that it's not all rainbows and butterflies, you let yourself be authentic, real, and vulnerable. You put your guard down when you need to, cry when you need to, and laugh when it's all just so ridiculous you don't know what else to do. That honesty is a great choice for our mental health while also sending out a lifeline to another mom who needs to know she isn't alone. That's an enormous gift. Thank you for that.

And how about the choices you have made to invest in yourself? You've spent time going to school, learning new skills, asking questions, and picking up a book on career fulfillment even when you barely have time to floss your teeth!

Along the way in your life, you have made great choices to help yourself become who you are today. You didn't wake up one day and just were a doctor/lawyer/candlemaker/teacher/project manager/business owner/paralegal. You worked for every single one of those things. You made time when there was none, you made sacrifices when things got hard. That was all you, making choices.

Tying this all together, you've also chosen to acknowledge that the choices you make for your career are not just yours to own now that you have children counting on you. Every step you take, every move you make, you are thinking about other people. And you're not just thinking about them, you're carefully considering the details of their lives and futures and intertwining them with your own.

How incredible is that? Think about it. We're born with survival instincts to look out for ourselves, and I will stand by the fact that we do still need to be a little selfish to make sure we keep our heads on straight, but as mothers, we are also born with a protective instinct. We turn that protective instinct into actions for our families, and rather complicated ones at that. You're there standing up for your kids' learning styles in School Committee meetings, stepping out of your comfort zones to request flexible work arrangements so you can be there for soccer games, and changing your goals to be inclusive of a family instead of an individual. That's huge! What choices! Kudos to you for keeping this crazy circus tent upright and thriving. I'm going to walk the talk and take some of those kudos for myself too. This stuff is hard, and I'm proud as all get up for doing it.

Take a minute to think about all your great choices and give yourself the credit you deserve! Write them down, draw little stars next to them, own those wonderful choices and how they brought you right here in this moment. You could go write down the not-so-great choices and mistakes when you reach the end of this chapter too, and if you feel like you need to do that to own your choices go ahead. But at the very least write down the good ones, please, and then go celebrate all you've accomplished as a parent and professional. I'll be right here, toasting you and your achievements, choices, and the personal responsibility you've taken in this wild ride we call life. You're making the world better for all of us.

————

I'll admit I was being a touch ridiculous with Norah's tiny one-year-old self when I told her to own her choices. However, I do like the "own your choices" line in parenting and how it relates to our lives as adults. I want my kids to grow up to be people who own up to their mistakes, take control of their circumstances, and have an awareness of how their actions impact others. I want them to choose the right thing when it gets hard and celebrate themselves for the good choices they've made. I want that for you too.

A word of warning though: teaching your kids to own their choices can come back to bite you.

"Buddy, why did you draw all over your arms with a marker on our way to school?" – Me

"Because I make my own choices. This was a choice I made for myself." – Jack, 3 years old

Owning Your Choices

The Good

Let's focus on the good stuff. What are some of the great choices you have made in your life so far?

The Bad

Notice how this section is smaller? That's on purpose because focusing on the good is more motivating! We've all made bad choices though, so if you want to write them down go for it. Make sure you also include what you learned from that choice though.

The Ugly

This section is reserved only for your worst middle school fashion faux pas. I'll go first with brown corduroy overalls... Yikes.

IF EVERYONE JUMPED OFF A BRIDGE, WOULD YOU?

We are deep into the bathroom humor stage in our house. From everything I've googled, this is a very common stage for little kids because potty training takes up a big part of their lives, and also farts sound funny. Another big reason why many conversations center on bathroom humor is the natural inclination for groups of three-year-olds to get into "who can be the silliest" battles. Without access to sarcasm or puns just yet, three-year-olds tend to fall back on toilet jokes as their shtick of choice.

One week at preschool, the battle of the silliness got particularly out of hand and Jack was sent home with a poor report about not listening and using bathroom words in a non-bathroom setting. When it comes to school behavior, Glen and I are a tad intense because we both wore shiny pairs of goody-two-shoes throughout our K-12 years. I can remember in exact detail the two times I got in trouble at school. TWO. To this day, I will claim the kid I kicked had it coming and I wasn't talking too much in class, that was Brian. Glen probably never got in trouble because he was a golden child and too busy playing soccer or rescuing puppies. Except there is the one terrifying story he tells about tying a block of ice to the back of a car and riding on it, but I don't think he got caught.

In any case, when Glen and I heard that Jack got in trouble at school we didn't take it all that well. It was a blow to our parental egos more than anything else because honestly, the kid was three. Calm down. Still, we had high expectations of our kids and we were very unhappy. The conversation went something like this:

"Jack, you know you aren't supposed to be using bathroom talk at school. It's not funny. Why are you doing that?"

"My friends were doing it too."

"I don't care what your friends are doing, why are YOU doing that?"

"It's just funny. We were laughing. Everyone else was too!"

"It's not funny and it doesn't matter what everyone else was doing! Focus on you! GAH, no TV. No toys. Sit in time out! Write an apology letter! Or make an apology picture! GO! Arghhhhhh."

We turned into pirates at the end there.

Somehow neither Glen nor I used the classic parent line "If everyone else jumped off a bridge would you do it too?" This was the right choice though because you shouldn't put ideas about jumping off things into a three-year-old's head. We were leaning hard into the same point, though; just because Nate, Jordan, and Arjun are spitting rhymes about butts and tackling each other on the playground doesn't mean you should. Be your own person. Make your own choices. Make better choices. You LOVE making choices.

Norah's not getting off the hook on this one either. The way she likes to incorporate bathroom talk into a conversation is by way of song though. This makes it harder to come down on her because you think she is doing an adorable rendition of "Tomorrow" from *Annie* and then all of a sudden the poop will come out tomorrow. Like any younger sibling, she is picking up this habit from her older sibling. And like any older sibling, Jack eggs her on because a) he thinks it's funny and b) he's psyched that our frustration is about to be divided by two. My girl is fiercely independent, but she's not immune to following the crowd either. I don't think any of us are.

Glen and I are still learning how to curb the bathroom humor and the "everyone is doing it" mindset with our kids, but there has been one thing that has worked well. When Jack earned his television privileges back after the preschool debacle, he and Norah plopped down on the couch for some *Word Girl*, a TV show on PBS about a cartoon super-hero whose superpower is her vocabulary because PBS is adorable. (She can also fly because even PBS knows there's only so much riveting television you can create from a cartoon saying "Stop right there, villain!") Most days when the cartoons come on Glen and I hightail it out of the room to go try to do something productive, but we must have been super exhausted that day because we were both on the couch when Word Girl announced her word for the day was "willpower."

Ah-ha! That's a good word! It's one of those words like "networking" that when you break it down into its parts it gets better. I "will" have the "power." Kids love having power! Thank you Word Girl and writer of the English language, you gave us a new way to tackle this problem.

After the show, we had a little chat with Jack about willpower, inspiring him to take on the next day like Word Girl, ready to do what is right. The next week as we dropped Jack off at school we gave him a big hug, asked him to lift his hands high in the air, and say "I can do it!" Then we gave him a high five for willpower. I don't know if it was the superpower, or the personal responsibility, or the high five, but it worked. Jack started finding different ways to have fun at school and the good reports were rolling back in. One day his teacher even told me that she overheard Jack say to his friends "No, I'm not going to do that. I want to tell my mom I had a good day." Oh my goodness, all the heart eyes emojis and parent of the year trophies. And all the donations to PBS.

———

This is a teeny tiny example of using willpower to combat peer pressure in your life and I know this conversation with my kids is far from over. Jack and Norah are still little and cartoons are not going to help us in all of the peer pressure, "but everyone's doing it," "just let me live my life!" conversations we're yet to have over their childhood and adolescence. Growing up is hard, cultivating the willpower to do what is right versus what is popular is hard. Honestly, I have a stress headache just thinking about those future conversations, proving yet again that this is in no way a parenting strategy book. If you can recommend a good one of those that will help me teach my children not to skip school and sneak bottles out of the liquor cabinet that would be great.

What I can help you with is flipping this conversation over to dealing with adult peer pressure in our lives and careers. "Peer pressure? As adults? We're in our 30's and 40's and far too evolved and mature for that nonsense!" you yell at me from across the room. "But are we though? Really?" I yell back. Then we both stop yelling at each other because the yelling wasn't necessary and we sit down and have a very civilized conversation about peer pressure while drinking tea and eating crumpets. Meanwhile, our children have run off to destroy the quaint cafe I've just decided we're all sitting in right now which is rather unfortunate because the place is adorable and there are a lot of breakables...

As we have our chat, we both agree that adults generally are not walking around making up songs about poop because the woman in the office next to us is doing it. For the most part, adulthood has shaken that level of silly right off of us. However, every day we are managing real or perceived pressure from people in the same life stage as us to do or not do something (read: peer pressure.) "Everyone is doing it" may not be the vocalized reason why we do things, but those feelings are very much there as we go about our lives making choices and worrying about the Judgey McJudgersons. What will people think of me if I choose to keep working after my kids are born? What will people think of me if I choose to stay home with my kids full time? Perhaps I should *Lean In* if everyone else successful in the business world is doing it? Perhaps I should be at home doing color-sorting exercises for my toddler with pom-poms if everyone I see on social media is doing it?

I can easily type these feelings out because they are my own. What does everyone else, including but not limited to my coworkers, my friends, my neighbors, my family, and that lady in Target, expect from me? Should I be doing something different or want something different because "everyone" is doing it even if I don't want to do that? Pressure, pushing down on me, pressing down on you, no mom ask for.

So how do we shake all our sillies off when it comes to worrying about what everyone else is thinking and doing? How can we put on our big girl panties and say, "No, I'm not going to jump off of that bridge with you. I'm going to stay right here doing what is right for me/working towards another goal I have set for myself in my career/raising my kids as I see fit whether you think that's correct or not." The long and short of it? It's hard and you'll second-guess yourself constantly, but that doesn't make it any less necessary.

———

For me, the fear of "everyone is doing it" started to rear its head years before I started blogging or had my own businesses. Thanks to my one-line-a-day journal I have proof! Journal Entry: September 2014: "I wonder what it would be like to be a comedy writer as a second career. That would be so much fun." Notice that I didn't say anything about actually going for that goal as a second career. I used words like "wonder" and "would be" instead of "going to" and "will be" even in my private journal. I was nervous to talk about the thing I wanted to do even when just talking to myself!

I know exactly what I was thinking at the time too. Stay the course here, lady. You chose a major, you chose a grad school, you chose this life and mapped it out. Having a steady career that relates directly to your degrees is the right thing to do and that's what everyone else is doing, so keep those crazy thoughts to yourself.

Yet day after day and year after year, writing funny things kept coming back up. My journal entries started to get more entertaining, I wrote a killer matron of honor speech, and I started analyzing the writing on comedy specials and sitcoms. There was something brewing right there on the surface but I was too afraid to tap into it fully because I was in my 30s, had kids, and felt like doing anything other than what was written on my diplomas would be out of bounds.

But then I met our friend Kenzie from way back in the prologue of this book. Kenzie could have looked around and decided to do what everyone thought she should do and be who everyone thought she should be, but that would mean denying who she was born to be. It would also mean being miserable. Instead, she courageously stepped forward onto a different bridge and made a jump of her own so that she could live her best and most fulfilled life. In comparison to the major life changes Kenzie took on in pursuit of her happiness, my desire to write funny words for someone else to read but not talking about that dream with anyone seemed utterly ridiculous.

As a result, I slowly started to build my own bridge by creating a blog, and then telling people about that blog, and then advertising the blog to find more readers. What would people think of my writing? What would people think of me asking people to read my writing? I didn't know and I wish I could say I didn't care, but I cared a lot. I didn't have any evidence to say that my friends would think I had my head in the clouds with this writing business, and there was no one at the office saying I couldn't be funny in my free time. Yet I still felt this imaginary pressure of other people's expectations. Plus when I took a glance around it seemed like everyone had these steady, stable, traditional jobs so I felt better hanging out on their bridge.

If I looked more closely though, other people were walking off the beaten path. Lots of people. Remember networking buddy, Amanda? She had left her nonprofit job to start her own businesses. I had a coworker living a double life between higher education and sketch comedy who eventually packed up and moved to LA to pursue comedy full-time. I had a neighbor taking a leave of absence from her job to run for political office. They were all there, doing something a bit different, facing the Judgey McJudgersons who may, or may not, have thought their "non-traditional" paths made sense, and then they just kept on doing their thing.

These people weren't magical unicorns, they simply had the willpower needed to follow their own paths and they remembered that in the adult world, peer pressure is often more of the imagined variety. Kate isn't telling us that she won't be our friend anymore if we pursue a new career path. We just think that maybe she won't or that she'll think you're being weird. In reality, Kate might think you are being weird for a second, but then she'll go back to worrying about what everyone else at the office thought about her new lipstick. We're self-involved, remember?

———

One of my coaching clients, who we'll call Lila, was dealing with this in a big way when deciding whether or not to leave a career in higher education to pursue building her own business. When Lila and I talked through her worries about leaving the field she had dedicated so much of her career to, other people entered the conversation many times. This rang some familiar bells so we started to break down who on that list of other people actually mattered to her. Lila's husband was supportive of her making a change, her friends and family just wanted her to be happy, and those colleagues who might think she is making a mistake? Well, that was still a big maybe since she hadn't talked to them about it. Also, if some of her colleagues disagreed, they realistically wouldn't worry about it for long and there was a good chance she wasn't going to stay in close touch with all of them if she left her job. That realization, along with the realization that moving on from that group of people didn't bother her much was freeing.

The big takeaway for me and for the people I've worked with as we soul searched and peer pressure analyzed—we all need willpower. Because whenever you are making the conscious decision not to jump off the bridge, or to jump off an entirely different bridge than "everyone else," there is going to be a lot of temptation to change your mind in favor of what everyone else is doing because that seems "right."

"Everyone" may be staying at home with their children. "Everyone" is climbing the corporate ladder. "Everyone" is a momtrepreneur. Not jumping off a particular bridge can sometimes feel scarier than jumping, because you suddenly feel kind of lonely on that bridge, even if you really like your bridge! Plus doing your own thing may not lead to the smoothest road, that's for sure. It will take a lot of willpower to stay true to yourself, but if something about following the crowd around you doesn't feel right and you hear a little voice telling you not to jump off that bridge, listen to the voice. A good life filled with meaningful work, time to do what you love, and time to be with who you love is worth it.

When you wrap up this chapter, write down the people in your life whose opinions actually matter to you. The list might start long because you have a lot of friends, family members, and acquaintances you'd like to look upon you approvingly. You're quite popular which I understand. In our time together at that cafe, you held up your end of the conversation swimmingly and you have lovely table manners.

You do need to take another pass at your long list with a critical eye though. Then you're going to start crossing off some names or just circling the top ones in case you're worried about lending someone this book and they see their name crossed off. That might be awkward. What you should be left with is a shortlist of the few people in your life you need to hold yourself accountable to. Your kids are probably on that list and your spouse or partner along with one or two other people, maybe. Everyone else still matters a ton, this isn't a "who do you love" list, but those people don't have a say in your career and life choices.

Does it feel kind of freeing to you, too? I hope so. Fly, you beautiful bird, fly!

———

I mentioned earlier that Norah is fiercely independent, despite some bathroom humor follow the leader. She potty-trained months ahead of her classmates because she wanted to do it herself. We also often find her hanging out in her room by herself reading books on her bed, not bothered in the least by what everyone else is doing. This lady even rode a bike without training wheels two months after she turned four! I could list about a dozen other examples, but the one that sticks out to me the most was the time during Dr. Seuss Spirit Week at school when Norah reminded me how important it is to be authentically you. On Hat Day, the rest of her classmates were wearing baseball hats and sun hats. There were even a few princess tiaras.

Not my Norah, though. She insisted on rocking a plush Daniel Tiger head from her Halloween costume and telling everyone that she was going to be Daniel Tiger when she grew up. She didn't care what Lucy or Aiden were wearing; Hat Day can be very open to interpretation if you let it. I love that her interpretation was uniquely Norah, and involved her career passions. Someone actually IS Daniel Tiger for their job, so why the heck not?

Regardless of what everyone else is doing, own your hat. Own your bridge. I'll be over here cheering you on from my bridge, seriously wondering why on Earth people choose to bungee jump because that seems terrifying, but supporting their choices all the same.

CHAPTER 11 NOTES

Whose opinions truly matter to you?

Remember, this is not a list of everyone you know, or even everyone you love. This is a list of who factors into the decisions you are going to be making for your life and career.

Hint: It's not going to be a long list!

ARE YOU FEELING JEALOUS?

The grass is always greener on the other side.
The green-eyed monster.
Green with envy.
It's not easy being green.

*T*he last one might have been Kermit...but he's right. It's not easy being green with jealousy. I know my kids can speak to this, and they have spoken to me about this, at length, when one of them is getting more attention or gets the better milk cup. Don't even get me started about the time the dog wanted to sit with Norah instead of with Jack. We're still dealing with that one.

I was worried about sibling jealousy well before we got to milk cup squabbles or dog custody battles though. It started the moment I found out I was pregnant with Norah. Jack was six months old at the time and my fear that he was going to fly into a jealous rage and start doubting our commitment to him was probably quite unfounded. However, as a first-time mom about to become a second-time mom in the span of two years, I was swimming in a sea of self-doubt. How could I care for each of my children equally? Not love, I felt strongly I could love them both, but how could I be there for them as much as they both needed? I was going to have two babies in my house with no idea of how to juggle it all. Do they make "World's Most Incompetent Mother" mugs or were my children going to have to have those custom made? My word, I'm such an inconvenience already...

With no crystal ball to look into and an old Magic 8 Ball that was being terribly noncommittal, we simply had to wait and see how this all played out. The first non-imaginary hurdle was "Umm...what do we do with Jack if I randomly go into labor and no one is here to watch him? Bring him along to the hospital and watch him be horrified while Mommy curses the beauty of childbirth?" Fortunately, I was feeling a bit off the Friday evening before Norah was born and my mom hopped in her car to drive an hour to our house, just in case. I went into labor within ten minutes of her walking in the door. It's like Norah knew her brother was all set and it was her turn. What a considerate kid.

Skipping ahead past pushing another human out of my lady parts, "suddenly" we were a family of four. Looking at this tiny baby girl was magic, and I had this overwhelming sense that Jack had made us a family and Norah had made us complete. (Cue hormonal sobbing.) Less than 24 hours later, Jack, at age 15 months, came to the hospital to meet Norah, accompanied by my parents. As we awaited his arrival, we didn't know what to expect. Would he be scared of the hospital room? Think Norah was a baby doll? Wonder why there weren't more snacks?

Donning a very official-looking "Big Brother" shirt, Jack came into the hospital room with a big balloon and the phone numbers of at least four doctors and nurses. True to form, his first request was for a snack, but then he came to sit with us on the hospital bed to meet his baby sister. Jack grinned ear-to-ear, softly patted Norah's head, and then reached out to hug her and give her a kiss. Every worry I had about having two kids well under two melted away. Everything was going to be okay. More than okay. They had each other and it felt amazing knowing we could give them that gift. Feelings!

After we brought Norah home from the hospital the next day, it was more of the same. Hugs, kisses, and snacks. As they have grown up, their affection for each other continues. Sometimes it's super sweet, and usually it's a little aggressive. Like a love hug tackle.

They get jealous of one another for sure though; that fear was not at all unfounded. Who is getting more attention (even negative attention, go figure), who gets to sit on the "chicken house side" of the car (which is a whole other story), whose turn it is to pick the TV show on Saturday morning... The jealousy is usually mitigated by the fact that these two love each other more than anything in the world though. Well, besides snacks.

———

I wonder a lot about how my kids' relationship will change over the years and how jealousy will play a part in that. We outgrow a lot of things as we age, like pacifiers, shoes, and the need for the Mickey Mouse water bottle, but do we ever really outgrow jealousy? From my experience as an adult, I'm fairly certain that we don't.

When Glen and I were struggling to start our family, I was jealous of every woman I passed on the street with a protruding belly. As the months went by and my life was marked by ovulation tests, two-week waits, periods, and miscarriages, the envy became all-consuming. Anyone reading this whose trying-to-conceive experience turned into a brutal journey is probably nodding along and feeling a tad uncomfortable nodding along. We want to be genuinely happy for others, jealousy doesn't feel good, but sometimes being happy for someone who has what you want is incredibly difficult.

The feeling is amplified when we feel like we don't have control to change our situation because we spend much of our lives feeling like we have at least some semblance of control. We choose our friends, our college, our major, our jobs, our apartments, our spouses. I think I'm so down with the "own your choices" philosophy because I like having control. "Control freak" is one way to put it; "aspiring ship captain" is perhaps another.

As little control I had over my fertility, I had even less control over other people. None really. It's not like I really wanted to control other people but it sure would have felt a lot better if I could have pressed pause on the world so I wasn't staring down a hallway of what I couldn't have. While fertility provides one example of adult jealousy out in the wild, there are plenty of others. It's everywhere. Keeping up with the Joneses, making our lives Pinterest perfect, and oh boy... Instagram filters! There are constantly opportunities to compare, measure, and wonder why your life doesn't look like her life. In "mom culture" we have started to talk about this kind of jealousy a lot and there is a good counterbalance of hot mess express social media that helps us feel a little less alone with our Cookie Monster cupcakes that look like melted blue demons. I'm glad documenting our epic failures is a thing in the mom world. Perfection is boring and unrealistic.

We don't often share our failures when it comes to career stuff though. No one is posting on LinkedIn about the promotion they didn't get or sharing their quarterly losses. Instead, rejection emails get quickly filed away, we toss our resumes in the recycle bin, and we put on a brave face for our friends and coworkers. Or we simply don't talk about it at all. Yet, the jealousy that comes with seeing others get where we want to be is still there, and it's a natural feeling.

Before we became mothers we had set goals for ourselves and our careers. After we became mothers we still had goals for ourselves and our careers. For some of us, those goals changed; for others, they stayed the same but suddenly they felt much more complicated because life got complicated. So now we are all working hard to achieve our goals, climb the ladder, or reach a milestone, and for any number of reasons, systematic, circumstantial, or "whelp, that's just the way the cookie crumbles" you may not get there as quickly as the person to your left or right. You can't always get what you want, at least not exactly when you want it, and that doesn't feel good.

Yet it's important to not let that green feeling turn us blue. (Come on, give me that one. It was adorable.) As my daughter can attest, pouting gets you nowhere in life, except maybe a time out to change your attitude. And while that little lower lip flip looks awfully cute on her, I'm sorry you can't pull it off in your 30s and 40s. I've tried, unsuccessfully. Instead of a time out, which sometimes as a parent sounds lovely actually, let's dive into some more parenting lessons we teach our kids to deal with career jealousy in a way that is healthy, productive, and sets you on the path towards your own success.

Keep Practicing

The first lesson to help manage jealousy, keep practicing. Is your kid jealous of their sibling because they won the race, made the team, or brought home the A+? As a parent, you remind your bummed out kid of their unique skills, but you also encourage them to keep practicing, keep trying, and figure out how they can achieve their goal next time. Good advice, huh?

What if the kid and their sibling were two coworkers competing for the same promotion instead? For story-telling's sake, we'll call them Jamie and Jane. Both Jamie and Jane bust their buns at the office, but Jane has also been brushing up on her financial skills with online courses. Plus she has been reading about the company's competitors in trade publications and can speak to how they are approaching international expansion. Jamie and Jane are both good candidates, but Jane gets the edge because she has a broader understanding of the company. So Jamie missed the boat on this promotion, and she's pretty upset.

However, instead of letting the green-eyed monster get her down for too long, she'll work towards the next promotion and fill the skills gap by taking courses, listening to podcasts, and reading books and articles. Jamie is a busy mom, but so is Jane, and these are all brain muscle flexing and career-advancing activities Jane did that Jamie can very comfortably partake in from her couch while forgoing rewatching another rerun of *The Office*.

As much as I also love watching Jim and Pam fall in love, this will be a better use of her time, at least right now while she has a big goal to chase. And it's a much better use of Jamie's time than creating a Jane dartboard or typing angry letters to her boss that she will never send.

Try Something New

Next lesson, try something new. Try new things is a lesson we push on our kids from the earliest of days. Time to try a new vegetable, try a new sport, try to learn addition, try to listen the first time. Trying new things is fun, hooray! Plus when we push ourselves out of our comfort zones we grow as people and start to appreciate more of this big old world we're living in.

We do tend to get a bit more set in our "ugh, I don't like asparagus" ways into adulthood though and it holds us back. Have you been plugging away in the same role for years and it's... well... fine, but you would love to feel more than fine? There's this woman you see at daycare pick up who looks like she is lit from within and is bounding up the stairs with the energy of seven toddlers after birthday cake. What's giving her that pep in her after work step? Is she that energized by her work and life that the positive vibes keep rolling throughout her day? You want to feel like that! Truth in advertising, maybe it's a fourth cup of coffee at 4 PM, but it could be because she is doing work she truly loves, and it could be time for you to make a change in your job too.

There are a few different ways you can take your work from fine to good to great that don't all involve finding a new job altogether. Like we've talked about, when I was feeling like everything was fine at work but not great, trying something new by taking on more is exactly what propelled me forward. I sought out more opportunities to write articles for the Harvard Business School career websites and while my plate was fuller, I was also happier! Making that ask to make my workday go from fine to good allowed me to take my career from good to great as a business owner. Now Harvard is a key client of mine in my business, a business that checks off all of my career and life criteria, and that never would have happened if I didn't try something new in my day job.

Another way to love the job you're with when it's not the job you love is to think about how you could help someone else. Go back to the Career Sweet Spot exercise we did way back in chapter two and see what value you could add to others and bring some of that into your day job. You'll get a burst of positive energy from mentoring a new hire, volunteering your time for a cause that's important to you, or teaching your team something new. I recommend this strategy to my coaching clients often and it's incredible to see the mindset shifts they come back with and how they see themselves differently. Helping someone gives you a huge boost of confidence in your ability to teach, lead, and inspire change. That's going to ripple over bigtime into your career and help push you forward.

Speaking of confidence, you may simply want to try putting on some lipstick. Don't worry, I'm not getting anti-feminist on you, you do not in any way have to wear lipstick if that's not your jam, but hear me out.

Being stuck in a career jealousy rut can drag you down and impact other areas of your life making you feel blah. When I felt blah and needed a creative jolt, I spent a month wearing bright red lipstick into the office. It was a bold choice for sure and I felt uncomfortable wearing it the first day since my makeup routine is pretty minimal and happens in the parking lot, but then the lipstick started feeling natural. I began wearing it with confidence and feeling put together in a way that I hadn't since my kids were born. Others noticed the change, in a good way.

One conversation went like this. "It's like we're just starting to see this other side of you, Becca. With the red lipstick in the office and the jokes on social media, I didn't know that part of you was there!" That part of me was there all along and now that I let my coworkers see it they could truly see me as someone itching to be more creative at work. This wasn't a "putting lipstick on a pig" situation, it was a "putting lipstick on a lady who wanted to feel authentic" situation, and that energy I put out attracted the energy I wanted to bring in. This seemingly simple change, which again, was lipstick for me but might be a blazer, glasses, upright posture, funky sneakers, no makeup, or purple hair for you, can make a huge difference.

You can also try something new by making a big change. A jumping off your own bridge change! A breaking all the rules change! Or maybe it's a big change that doesn't require bridges or rule-breaking but does require you to put your hat in the ring for a new job and leave a position you've felt comfortable in for years. If that's you, stay tuned for Part 5 of this book and we're going to dive into job search logistics to help you get where you want to go.

Change, big or small, can be scary. Even as someone who loves creativity and newness, I would also quite happily live in the same pair of gray sweatpants for the rest of my days. I have never dyed my hair a different color or moved out of my time zone or even briefly considered wearing a jumpsuit. Like many people, I like to be comfortable. However, comfortable can be dangerous, like the time the UPS driver told me to "get well soon" but I wasn't actually sick, I just hadn't changed out of my pajamas on a work-from-home day and it was 3:00 PM. Or when I nearly drove away from a networking event because I couldn't find a parking spot on my first pass around the lot and was not so secretly relieved. If I hadn't tried something new though and circled that parking again, I wouldn't have met some great people, including some of my future clients. Comfortable is great, but change can be great too.

Don't Cheat

Onto the next jealousy related parenting lesson, don't cheat. I don't need to tell you how hard it is to teach toddlers and preschoolers how to play board games. There is waiting, there are turns, there is the very real and understandable desire to win. I get it, kiddos; I also want to have my hungry hippo gobble up the most marbles. However, it's on us as parents to make sure the kids don't scoop up the marbles with their hands, or flip over a bunch of memory cards at the same time, or peek open their eyes while they are counting for hide-and-seek. We need to teach them fair play and good rules so they grow up without the mindset of "cheat to win."

Not cheating to win should seem like the simplest rule on the career development side, but it's honestly not. So many people who are feeling jealous of someone's success feel tempted to cut corners, steal ideas, or tell one too many white lies to help carve their own path. For example, a friend of mine, along with everyone in her organization, received a full PowerPoint presentation that reminded people not to steal money from the company, because it had really happened. A handful of employees had felt entitled, or greedy, or desperate, or jealous enough to steal what wasn't theirs. These full-grown adults were trying to cheat to win.

Unfortunately, that might not seem that outlandish to you because we've grown up in the era of Lehman Brothers and doping scandals. We're surrounded by adults trying to game the system and skip past the frosted flakes forest in Candy Land. It's not cool at all, but it's also very common.

Maybe you're tempted to find the easy way towards achieving your goals, too. The jealousy bug bit you and you want to jump ahead by taking credit for a colleague's idea or skipping important steps on a project to save time.

No one is perfect, and it's natural to take the "do whatever it takes" mindset too far, especially when you are trying to manage so many areas of your life. We joke about "adulting," but honestly, it is hard. We set expectations for ourselves that are unrealistic and then beat ourselves up when we can't find a quick way to achieve them.

The antidote to this, be kind to yourself. Take your time towards achieving your goals or figuring out what you want to be when you grow up. There might be Band-Aid solutions that feel like finding the cheat codes, but they don't last. It's a process. Stay the course. No cheating.

Be Patient

One more lesson to help curb the green-eyed monster, be patient. Patience is like the secret ingredient for raising children, and it's a compliment that when received can feel both fantastic and maybe a little backhanded. It's lovely to be called patient when you are painstakingly helping your kid with an educational craft or teaching them their letters. Look at you, all patient! But then when your kid is losing his or her ever-loving mind at a birthday party, being told that you are "so patient" is basically like saying "Yup, glad that's not my problem right now. That kid? Yikes."

Throughout my life, I've struggled with being patient, and instead, I tend to operate with a sense of urgency all the time. I don't like to be late, I don't want to twiddle my thumbs, I want to get where I'm going and be there. What my housekeeping lacks in attention to detail it makes up for in efficiency. I consistently stop the microwave at 11 seconds left because it's probably warm enough and I need to get a move on. I like to get things done and I like it when others get things done too. Patience is hard for kids, but it can be hard for adults too. For your career, it can be very helpful to get a little perspective on this though from those who have waited it out.

By this point, we all know that J.K. Rowling received a stack of rejection letters for *Harry Potter* before hearing yes. Did you also know that Abraham Lincoln lost election after election before getting his face on the five-dollar bill? And your neighbor, she didn't turn a profit on her small business until year three and worked two other jobs in the meantime. The really good stuff, it takes time.

Or perhaps your career wait is less about someone giving you a chance, and more about waiting for your light bulb moment that helps you figure out what you want to be when you grow up. There are hundreds of stories of successful people who didn't figure it all out at age 18. Vera Wang designed her first dress at age 40. Julia Child released her first cookbook at age 50. Painter Grandma Moses started painting at age 78, after spending her career working on a farm and cleaning houses. The doors to success don't automatically lock-up by a certain age or time. You aren't Cinderella, darling. Stop looking at the clock. Instead, keep working while you are waiting, allowing yourself to learn and grow along the way, and feel assured of the fact that there is no such thing as an overnight sensation, for you or for anyone else.

———

There's another way to overcome career jealousy, which doesn't align perfectly with lessons we teach our kids but it's my book so we're going rouge, is to understand that everyone fails. Everyone. The person whose career you are coveting, she failed on her way there. 110% guaranteed.

Let's say this book is a major commercial success someday and the person you are feeling jealous of is me. That's a weird sentence to write, but it's going to help make my point so I'm willing to be awkward about this. On my way to this high-flying success I changed career paths twice in adulthood, I was turned down from too many jobs to count, I yelled at my kids when I could have been calm, I wore flared jeans way past the time they were cool and not because I was being ironic about it. I've failed. A lot.

However, Glen and I high five each other over failures. Literally. We're nerds and high five a lot, but we high five over failure specifically because it means we tried something new and that in itself deserves celebration. So we weren't surprised when at age four Jack wrote a song called "We learn from failure." The verses could still use some work but I swear Glen and I are going to retire in the Bahamas on that hot jam. At the core of our high fives and Jack's lyrics is the idea that I fall, you fall, we all fall. Then we get back up and we try again. Or we try differently because we learned. Or we turn that fall into an awesome somersault and raise our hands in triumph at the end pretending like we meant to do it. Perhaps that somersault makes it into an interview story about overcoming an obstacle and showing adversity? Valuable right?

This is all to say that the person you are jealous of, they have failed too. Then they learned. Failure isn't fun but it's a really important part of the process.

———

One more note about jealousy. One night in the fall of 2018 I was feeling very jealous. Of George Washington.

As I was giving Jack and Norah a bath, Jack was a little mad at me because I got some water in his eyes. I told him it was just a mistake to which he replied, "I want a new Mommy and Daddy who don't make mistakes! Like George Washington. And Amanda Doherty."

I'm not quite up to snuff I guess. Not like the original POTUS. Or Amanda Doherty? Who is Amanda Doherty? Turns out she's his friend's mom, and according to my Facebook stalking she does seem pretty cool. I'll try not to be jealous though.

CHAPTER 12 NOTES

What can you control?

Life can be overwhelming sometimes (okay a lot of the times) but there will always be things we can control. What do you have full control over right now in terms of your life and career?

Examples: What jobs you apply for, which people you choose to connect with, how you spend your time after the kids are in bed, your attitude, etc!

PART IV

ON KEEPING MOMENTUM

Losing some steam as you go after your dreams?
Don't worry. You've got this!

I'LL CHECK ON YOU

*C*ertain childhood milestones are super exciting and extremely photographable. First tastes of solid food, first steps, first day of school - they are each filled with so much cuteness and they each use up their fair share of phone storage. Yet not all childhood milestones are created equal and there is one in particular that made me and Glen cry, and not in a "they are growing up so fast" way, but rather in a "this is terrible, please rewind time, I desperately need some sleep" kind of way. That milestone was moving our kids from their cribs into toddler beds.

Even though my law-abiding first-born never attempted to climb out of his crib, one day as Jack neared age three Glen announced that our little guy was getting a toddler bed. I reluctantly agreed that it was probably time, Glen broke out the tools for the crib to bed conversion, and I waited around knowing that my well-honed construction skill of "hold this piece of wood steady for a minute" would likely be needed at some point.

Spoiler alert, my big helper skills were utilized, but moving Jack out of his crib was a no good very bad decision, and not just because I'm useless with construction. If you need actual evidence that toddler beds are life ruiners beyond just my dramatic say-so, know that if you are considering making the switch from a crib to a toddler bed you can and should make this change if you are in any of the following situations:

1. You have decided that you hate sleep and would like to answer questions from a suddenly free to roam toddler at 2:30 AM.

2. You'd like to test your toddler's ability to withstand a 7-inch fall from their bed several times a night. The kid needs to toughen up.

3. You're questioning whether or not you should have a third kid and want to see what it's like to wake up eleventy million times a night again.

4. All intimacy in your marriage has died and it would be totally fine for your toddler to be awake at all times and able to walk into your bedroom unannounced.

5. You get lonely during nap time and would relish the opportunity for your child to stay in bed for 12 seconds midday and then rejoin you in the kitchen demanding apples cut "the right way."

6. You're considering getting new carpeting but haven't slept on it at the foot of your toddler's bed in a desperate attempt to have him stay there recently. You won't truly know how comfortable that carpeting is, or is not, until you try.

7. Your life is free from regret. So far you've made a lot of great choices. No questionable haircuts, decent looking resume, your walks have been free from shame. That's boring! Other people must find you insufferable. Take a chance and get your toddler out of that crib. It will make your memoir more sleep-deprived and more interesting.

Sounds like a lot of fun, right? Fortunately, we figured out pretty quickly that all Jack needed to not fall out of his bed was a bed rail, but naps were now a distant memory because he could easily escape the bed and there was no turning back.

Then the real kicker was that Norah, in true second child "I want to do that too" fashion, started imaging how her life would transform with a toddler bed shortly after Jack made his big move. If this had turned into a slow burn of attempted crib escapes we could have prepared, but one day after we put Norah into her crib, she looked up at us with amusement and easily hurdled over the crib railing with no warning. She even stuck the landing, tens across the board. "Maybe she'll just climb out that one time," we whispered into the universe, trying to invoke *The Secret*. Apparently, it takes a little longer for your hopes and dreams to be heard in the universe because 90 minutes later we were still trying to get Norah to sleep in her crib. There was lots of wine that night (just for me) and whine (for both of us.)

The next night, against our own best advice and for safety reasons, we converted Norah's crib to a big kid bed too. "Hooray!," said no one. "This is so exciting!" no one cheered. Our lack of enthusiasm was rewarded with our low expectations being met. Actually, they weren't even met, we had set the bar too high. Now Norah was coming out of her room every hour on the hour, like precious, maddening, zombie parent inducing clockwork.

Several days into this night time dilemma, I sleepwalked into a meeting with a coworker who also has two small kids. She asked how I was and instead of saying "Good!" I answered "Exhausted. Norah isn't staying in her bed and I don't think I am ever going to sleep again and everything is terrible. So, how are you? How's the family?" I'm very glad I used my honest words at that moment because my coworker's sister-in-law happened to be a child sleep consultant who knew the answer to my problem. Four simple words were about to save our family's sanity: "I'll check on you."

With professional sleep consultant advice in hand, that night I tucked Norah into her toddler bed and sat down next to her on the floor. After a few minutes, I got up and told her I was going to the bathroom and that I would come back to check on her, but I could only come to check if she stayed lying down in her bed. I left the room and came back one minute later, rewarding her trust. After a few more minutes I told her I was going to the bathroom again and left the room. A short interlude of hallway Instacrolling later and I came back to the room to check on her. It took three pretend bathroom breaks until she fell asleep. The next night we were down to two. After about a week we didn't need to sit on the floor at all. A simple "Sweet dreams, Norah. If you stay in your bed I'll come back and check on you" was all my little girl needed to feel comfortable staying put and falling asleep.

What this beautiful strategy boils down to are account-ability and trust. I was there for her, she could trust me, but I also held her accountable. If she didn't do the work of staying in her bed, then I couldn't help her by checking on her. I was on the sidelines as her coach, she was playing the game. We both had to put in the effort to make this work. (And I am eternally grateful it worked.)

———

When I think about the work I do as a career coach, it comes back to the same principles of "I'll check on you," trust and accountability. For example, I talk with coaching clients about how to create a networking strategy and have informational conversations with strangers, and they can trust that I'll offer sound advice, but they also know I'm not getting on the phone with the company for them. If they need me to hold them accountable by following up to see how their phone calls went and encouraging them to make more connections, I'm happy to help. It's their responsibility to do the work, but I'll check on them. Sports coaches, health coaches, career coaches - it's all the same deal. Listening, asking, guiding, advising, encouraging, and providing accountability.

If you are in a career rut and picked up this book to give you a boost, I hope it is doing just that. I hope that even one chapter has given you a nugget to instill in your life that will give your career development a kick start. However, if you haven't found that nugget yet, it might simply be this: Find a professional career coach who will check on you. A good career coach will sit on your hypothetical bedroom floor to be there with you and hash out your professional insecurities and career and life criteria. They will listen intently, ask insightful questions, and give you a dedicated space to figure all this out. They will check on you during a session to see how this process is making you feel, and then can check on you after to see how your next steps are going. Your coach isn't going to do the work for you, but she will be there for you and hold you accountable. That kind of accountability makes a big difference.

If you don't go the career coach route, that's fine. I won't be personally or professionally offended, but I'm not letting you off the accountability hook. Either is author Gretchen Rubin. In Rubin's book, *Four Tendencies*, she talks about a huge challenge—getting ourselves to do what we want.[1]

Maybe we know <u>exactly</u> what would make us happy, but something deep inside keeps us from doing that thing and it's our job to figure out what that is so we can overcome it.

Rubin outlines four different archetypes of people to help readers understand what kind of motivation and accountability they need in their lives. The four archetypes are Upholders, Questioners, Rebels, and Obligers. Upholders want a blueprint of what needs to get done and they are internally motivated, like the kid who wants the LEGO instruction manual and will get to work on her own. Questioners want justifications for why they should do something, like the kid who needs to know why we need to eat our vegetables. Rebels want the freedom to do something their own way, like the kid we are tempted to put on a leash. Lastly, Obligers need external accountability, like the kid who isn't going to clean his room unless you're standing by the door. Obligers tend to do what other people expect of them, but they don't follow through for themselves. It sounds kind of negative on its face, but a lot of people fall into the Obliger category, which is why group programs like Weight Watchers are so effective. It's why we show up for charity 5Ks that we signed up for with our friends instead of bailing to go have brunch. We like and often need other people to be cheering us on and checking in on us.

From a career perspective, let's say you want to get a promotion at work. The higher level of responsibility would make you feel proud, the extra salary would keep your family rolling in name brand Pop-Tarts, and the opportunity to do more challenging work is exciting. You know exactly what it would take for you to earn that promotion, too. You need to improve your public speaking, prove your leadership skills, and raise your hand to join cross-functional teams.

Someone with an Upholder mindset might make themselves a checklist and then cross things off one by one. However, someone with an Obliger mindset could have a hard time finding the motivation to go after the thing they want. Maybe they decide not to speak up in meetings so that others have more airtime, or they focus on their own work instead of trying something new because that's what their job description says. If you go a psychological level deeper, there are usually underlying reasons behind the excuses you make up in your head for behaving in this way. For example, you're afraid of what others will think about your ambition, you doubt your own abilities, or you don't want to feel uncomfortable.

If the Obliger archetype feels like you, a "you're good enough, you're smart enough" mirror pep talk in the morning may not be enough to give yourself the motivation to follow through on your goals. (We'll talk about those pep talks in another chapter though because they really can work.) Having someone else hold you accountable so that you feel the need to meet their expectations could work though. This might be a trusted mentor, your partner, or a good friend.

For me, it has been all of those people! I've had formal accountability partners by way of a monthly lunch with coworkers where we talk about our goals and fears, and I've had informal accountability partners with whom I exchange Facebook messages. Glen has been my accountability partner when I drag my heels on following through on the not so fun parts of running a business, like asking people for money or figuring out my taxes. He's not going to do it for me, but he'll be there to make sure I don't let it slide. While I can be an Upholder when it comes to making funny memes, there are other areas of life and business that I know my

Obliger is showing, and that's okay. Know yourself and what you need.

One of the big reasons this book is actually in your hands right now is accountability. Authoring this book was a huge career goal of mine, so I started telling people about it. I pitched the idea to close friends and family. I wrote about it on my blog. I talked about it with other writers. This was a way to see if the idea in my brain resonated with someone else's brain, but it was also a way to ensure that I wouldn't bail on the project.

Turns out that was a good thing because in the early days of writing my friend Lindsay sent me a message. "How's the book coming?" My response to Lindsay was going to be "slow" and that felt embarrassing. I could have listed out a trillion valid and another trillion not-so-valid excuses as to why the book was coming along slowly. I was focusing on building the blog to hone my craft. I needed a social media following to sell a book so I was making lots of memes. My children kept waking up in the middle of the night. I had gotten really into *GLOW* on Netflix...

At the end of the day though, I knew what my goal was and I had read plenty of time management books and success memoirs that told me exactly what to do so that I could achieve that goal - namely get my rear out of bed early to write before the kids woke up. I simply wasn't doing it. So instead of messaging Lindsay back right away, I set my alarm for 5:30 AM so that I could at least squeeze in maybe fifteen minutes of writing in the morning before the kids woke up. That worked. After a couple of days I changed the alarm to 5:15 AM and the pages of this book started to fill up. As I type this my alarm for the past two weeks has been on for 5:00 AM every day and that became one of those personal rules I mentioned earlier.

Did I always actually get out of bed at 5:00 AM? Of course not, one, because I'm human and two, because sometimes my children would sneak into our bed at night and I'd be pinned. However, even if I was up four days out of seven that was better than zero. Within two weeks of Lindsay's prompt to get moving I had written five chapters. All of that stemmed from accountability.

After two weeks I messaged Lindsay back to let her know how her question had kicked my behind into gear. Then she told me what I should have already known – 5:00 AM to 6:00 AM is when she had written most of her book too, a beautiful masterpiece on faith and family, *Don't Forget To Say Thank You: And Other Parenting Lessons That Brought Me Closer to God.*[2] Lindsay and I have had mutual friends for fifteen years, but it wasn't until I dove into writing that I found myself connecting with her regularly. Glen, my family, and other close friends are great cheerleaders and are so supportive of my career, but there is something uniquely important about having someone who has walked this path before check on me. Do you have a Lindsay in your life who has walked on the path you want to head down? If not, go find her, tell her about your goals, and tell her I said hi!

————

This was going to be the part of the book where I mailed it in and leaned on a "Webster's dictionary defines accountability as..." But Webster's a punk and he defines accountability as "the quality or state of being accountable." So, instead of this being a helpful paragraph, I got to call Webster a punk. Anyway, I think you get what accountability is all about, especially because as a parent you know exactly who you are accountable to at the end of the day - your kids.

It's our kids who are holding us accountable for raising them well, setting a good example, and keeping them safe. It's our kids that matter more to us than any professional achievement or career goal, despite how important those things are to us as well. Yet while the outside world may tell you that this sentiment, that our kids come first, may hold us back in our careers, I'm ready to fight the whole outside world on that. Boxing gloves on, let's do this.

There is something undeniably powerful about having little humans counting on you to do the right thing. You may be willing to let yourself down, but I know you're not willing to let them down for anything. It's how you're hardwired now as a parent. What that looks like in practice is staying up late at night worrying if you've prepared them well enough for kindergarten, and replaying your overreaction to a minor childhood transgression over and over. It looks like wearing the same underwear you've had for 10 years to save money to buy back to school clothes. It looks like showing up at the soccer game, and reading the bedtime stories, and playing Barbies when you'd rather take a nap.

Accountability to your kids can also look like something else though. It can look like having the motivation to get up every day to work your tail off bringing in the income your family needs. It can look like pushing yourself to do meaningful work you're proud of so that your kids will be proud of you too. It can look like refusing to give up on your dreams so that they learn not to give up on theirs. What employer wouldn't want someone with that kind of motivation and drive? What business couldn't thrive when it was powered by that kind of accountability?

This is all to say that I sincerely believe you don't need to choose between your career goals and motherhood - they are linked so strongly that one benefits the other. Your drive to be a great mother means that you are driven to provide for your family, in whatever ways your family needs most. Your drive to be great at work means that you are driven to show your children that success is possible. Your desire to prove to yourself that you can achieve a goal may just have you holding back tears as your four-year-old softly chants to herself "You can do this, Norah. You can do this." while attempting the monkey bars for the first time. You know, just as an example...

This comes off a little simplistic, I know. There are logistics to consider as you manage family life and work life, pesky little things like money and time, and we'll get into that because we have to. But those little humans who are trusting you to show them the way and holding you accountable for figuring out the tough stuff in life? Well, to absolutely butcher some Robert Frost, they could make all the difference.

CHAPTER 13 NOTES

Who holds you accountable for achieving your goals?

If you have someone in your life whom you trust to hold you accountable and will check on you, write their name below and then send them a text. Seriously, right now! Ask them to be your accountability partner so you can support each other and keep each other on track.

If you don't have someone, consider hiring a coach and make it someone you are comfortable with. I say this is in every single coaching consultation call, your coach has to be someone you trust and you can be honest with. If not, it won't work out.

Visit beccacarnahan.com to learn more about my career coaching practice and sign up for a consultation. I'm also happy to provide recommendations for other excellent coaches who could be the right fit for you.

YOU ARE SO BRAVE

I learned about bravery on June 16, 2018. Sure I had witnessed bravery before that point, and I had been brave myself from time to time (hello, birthing children!), but this day was a turning point. It happened exactly where you'd expect it to happen too, at a little kid's gymnastics class.

At the time, Jack and Norah were going to The Little Gym for gymnastics class each Saturday. In their classes they each learned how to walk on balance beams, climb rock walls, and do forward rolls. It was also a fabulous way to burn off some toddler/preschool energy. The Little Gym single-handedly saved my walls from being covered in small child rage crayon. It was worth every penny.

Each session lasts for about four months, and then at the end, there is a "Big Show." At the Big Show, the kids show off what they have learned, get to use their favorite gymnastic equipment, and then get rewarded with a medal. During the medal ceremony, the Olympic music comes on and the kids each have their moment in the sun with lots of clapping and cheering. Norah's Big Show was first that morning and she was having a blast climbing, swinging, and running. She's naturally athletic (I think, I don't know, she was two) so she had done a great job with all the new skills and activities over the past four months. There were smiles, and giggles, and an intense amount of cuteness until we got to the medal ceremony. Then things started to go rapidly downhill, or so I thought.

Norah found a seat on the mat, waiting her turn in line to get her medal. It's important to note that to her this wasn't just any medal. Jack had a Little Gym medal on his doorknob from last year and she had been pining over it for months. We had been telling her that she was going to get her own special medal at her Big Show if she worked super hard at gymnastics, so she knew what this was all about, and she had the eye of the tiger cub. That medal was hers. She waited patiently while a few kids went up to get their medals and we all clapped and cheered.

Then out of nowhere, Norah's face crumbled and she let out a terrified sob. Glen scooped her up and the poor thing just couldn't pull it together. She was beside herself, overwhelmed by the people, the music, and all the theatrics of the event. Norah looked at me with the saddest big blue eyes and said "Mommy, I scared."

I took Norah out into the hallway to help her catch her breath and through big sobs, she told me she wanted to go back into the class. I hesitated a bit but thought that we could try it and see if maybe her fear would subside after seeing a few more kids get their awards. Not so much. But through hiccups and splashy tears she still wanted to sit back down on the mat. So there we sat, me hugging her tightly and Norah hating everything but also showing more grit than most full-grown adults. This lady had no intention of leaving the class again. She was getting that medal.

The teacher looked at me before calling Norah's name and I kind of shrugged as if to say "Couldn't tell you what's going to happen here. Go for it, I guess?" She called Norah's name and my brave little girl stood right up and walked over to the podium and climbed the steps, tears streaming down her face the whole time. The medal was put over her head and she climbed back down and walked over for some mom snuggles. The tears didn't stop until well after the class was over and we went to the Dunkin Donuts next door. Because, well, donuts.

I felt awful at first. Should I have hugged her closer? Asked the teacher to get the medal later? Did I just traumatize my two-year-old and solidify a nomination as Worst Mother of the Year, toddler category? Yet as Norah sat happily with her donut, catching glances at the medal around her neck, I realized that she might be the bravest person I know. When was the last time I had been so terrified of doing something I wanted to do that I sobbed uncontrollably in public, and then did the thing anyway?

As she polished off the donut, I told Norah that I was so proud of her because she was courageous. She was scared but did it anyway. The very definition of bravery. She rubbed some blue icing into her hair and smiled because again, donuts. I knew there was going to be a battle royale to get that icing out of her hair later and I'd be back in my role as teacher and caregiver soon enough. For this moment though, she was very much in charge. She was the teacher, I was the student, and I felt so lucky to be her mom.

———

I'll always hold a special place in my heart for Norah's Little Gym bravery story because it gave me a serious kick in the pants. I needed to be like Norah and be a little braver, or maybe a lot braver in my life and career. It wasn't just the "go after the thing that makes you a little uneasy" kind of brave either. I had done that in my career, but those things didn't change my life trajectory. What I was seeking out was the "shake you to your core, cry on the way to the podium" kind of brave. The "have a dream, take a big risk, feel all the feels, wake up at night in a cold sweat" kind of brave. That kind of brave is the kind that reaps the big rewards and makes you better. I realized I owed that to my kids.

Looking back on my career to date, I could think of many examples in which I was being kind of brave. Making cold calls at the Celtics knowing I would be rejected nine times out of ten, or twenty. Applying for a job at Harvard Business School when I didn't have the required years of experience. Asking my boss for a flexible schedule so that I could attend graduate school. Leaving that job for a new job while in the middle of my graduate program, not knowing how I was going to manage to learn all new things all the time. Advocating for a higher salary. Starting my blog. Writing publicly about my miscarriages. These things were also scary in their own way and I'm proud looking back on them.

None of it was podium level though. I wasn't crying on the way to my cold calls, or breaking my way through almost paralyzing fear to ask for a raise. Everything had felt doable and low risk before. Becoming my own boss though, the thing I found that I desperately wanted, that felt risky. That felt nauseating. That felt "cry on the way to the podium if I ever work up the guts to pull myself off the mat" level brave. I was making quiet and slow progress in building a business with my blog, and there's nothing wrong with either quiet or slow. Those are completely legitimate ways to start a business. However, I knew I wasn't being as brave as I could be. Really being brave would mean cutting a hole in the safety net so that I could fly or fall instead of eternally swinging around in the in-between.

After more hemming, more hawing, and more talking in circles about it with Glen, I decided it was time. As I prepared to tell my manager that I was officially walking away from an incredibly stable job in 2020 in the middle of a global pandemic, my heart was pounding out of my chest. I wondered if this was a huge mistake, I wondered if I was "throwing away my career" in one single conversation. I had to do it though. Making this big decision was the right move for this stage of my life, and so I stepped up on the podium, cried a great deal, and owned it. I choked up as I talked about finalizing my last day and submitting my resignation letter, I cried as I cleared out nearly thirteen years of memories from my office, and I let big ugly tears fall as I listened to Boys II Men "It's So Hard To Say Goodbye" on the drive home that would lead me into self-employment.

I'm an emotional cat so it didn't surprise me that I cried, but I'm also glad I did. If this was my podium-level brave moment it was bound to be emotional. It was, and it was worth it.

———

Bravery in your career can manifest itself in many different ways. The "shake you to your core, cry on the way to the podium" kind of brave genuinely depends on what your personal podium is. Maybe it looks like mine and you're going to start a business of your own, taking all the risk and reward that comes with it. Or maybe your podium level brave looks like leaving your paying job to be a stay at home parent because that's what your heart is telling you to do and you're ready for the challenges and opportunities ahead. Perhaps your podium is a promotion, publishing a book, patenting an invention, changing industries, or being the first person who looks like you to hold the title of CEO.

The important thing to remember is that it is your podium, not mine. Not Lydia's, or Janet's, or Kimberly's. It's yours, so you need to define what it is and then own it.

Defining your podium can start with being honest with yourself, which is scary but hopefully less scary after you've read part one of this book! Then once you figure out what your thing is, your next level of bravery will be using your words to be that honest with other people to tell them about your goals and plan. Your bravery will then be about trying again when you fail, and when you fail again, and again. Or it might look like putting a big idea that you have poured your heart into onto the table, only to have it get shut down or laughed off the stage. All of that can be scary. However, if it means so much to you that it keeps you awake at night, that's podium level.

Throughout my career as a coach, I've had the privilege of witnessing podium level brave time and time again. One of my clients, who we'll call Andrea, found her podium level brave moment when she decided not to accept a job offer that didn't match up with her career and life criteria. It was terrifying, but she waited for the right job, and her wait paid off. Another client, Adam, said yes to a networking call with a stranger when it was the last thing in the entire world he wanted to do. However, Adam knew that networking could make a difference in his job search and he needed to try something different no matter how much that shook him to his core. Yet another coaching client, Kristin, found her podium level brave when she put herself out there to start a new business despite battling some serious impostor syndrome.

(We'll talk more about impostor syndrome in the next chapter. We'll also talk about vomit in the next chapter but that's unrelated.)

Sometimes bravery is about saying yes, not knowing exactly where that yes is going to take you but assuming it will probably be way out of your comfort zone. Other times bravery is about saying no, which can be terrifying because you are closing a door that could lead to some objectively great things. You might even get some side-eye from those who know and love you because "Why oh why would you close that safe and objectively great door?" Just remember it's your podium, your medal, and your donut and you can get that blue icing anywhere you want.

———

I'm not brave every day, but I'm learning. I'm learning by watching my kids get over their fear of going underwater. I'm learning by doing scary things like going to networking events and talking to strangers. I'm even learning to be brave by chasing bats out of my house!

One night I came downstairs from putting Norah to bed to find Glen standing in the living room with a blanket, cool as a cucumber, saying, "Oh hey, we're out of milk, and also there's a bat in our house." My two immediate thoughts were: One, can I pretend that he didn't just say that and go sit down with a glass of wine and watch *The Bachelor*? And two, all the curse words.

Googled instructions on "How to get a bat out of your house and out of your life" in hand, we ventured down into the basement where the bat was last seen. Creeping around the basement with an iPhone flashlight, and fully clothed but also wrapped in a towel for some reason, I was beyond terrified. Then, my loving husband had the nerve to say to me, "He's more scared of us than we are of him" but fast forward five more minutes, and my big, strong husband and I were both anxiously looking behind every nook and cranny of the basement both hoping to find and desperately hoping NOT to find this little devil rat with wings. Unfortunately, as I stood there scared and useless, I accidentally found the bat hanging out like he owned the joint up on the top of the wall.

"GLEN (in a harsh whisper). I found...the bat."

Glen geared up in gloves, a trash bag, and my least favorite Tupperware and got ready to scoop the bat. I continued to stand guard to make sure the bat didn't fly back up the stairs all the while giving myself a mobster-style bravery pep talk. "Protect the family, Becca. PROTECT THE FAMILY!"

The bat did not want to be scooped though. He wriggled his angry little body out of the Tupperware and started flying laps around the basement while I held up my towel and alternated between nervous laughter and yelling "AHH-HHHHHH!" Glen's reaction was way better though. It was like he was in a cage match with the bat, swearing a blue streak while chasing it around the basement with a blanket trying to catch the little rodent while also trying to avoid it like the plague.

Eventually, the blanket landed over the bat and took it down to the floor. Glen proceeded to drag the pile of blankets and towels covering the bat out the door into the pouring rain while I cheered enthusiastically "You're doing it! YOU'RE DOING IT!" As soon as the blankets were flipped outside to let the bat free, Glen slammed the basement door and locked it. You know, just in case bats are vengeful and have opposable thumbs.

The point of this story is to highlight how incredibly brave I am. It's also to remind you that bravery doesn't always look like painting your face half blue and shouting "They will never take our freedom!" Sometimes it looks like facing something small and ridiculous that scares you but doing it away. I bet you can do that, and I bet you can take on that podium too. You are so brave.

CHAPTER 14 NOTES

What is your big podium level brave goal?
Shout it out (and write it down!)

BELIEVE IN YOURSELF

*M*other's Day 2018 started at 1:43 AM in our house. With vomit.

Norah had seemed perfectly healthy the night before and in these early morning hours it appeared to be a boot and rally situation, but it was a two-parent level boot. Glen got her cleaned up while I changed the sheets. Then he got her settled back in for nighttime routine number two while I sat in bed knowing that I wouldn't fall asleep until my daughter was sleeping soundly again. To pass the time, I checked my phone.

Big mistake. Huge.

Right there at the top of my inbox was a big fat no, another one, and my bruised ego just couldn't take it. Over the past several months I had been sending articles to large websites to be considered for publication and it wasn't going well. I had received rejection email after rejection email and none of them were fun. Plus this particular rejection email came right after vomit.

Feeling defeated was not a very comfortable feeling as I've always walked around with what one might argue is an overabundance of self-confidence. I was the kid who felt confident raising my hand a lot, and the adult who could easily make fun of myself because I knew I could take the joke. I was even confident enough in my tweens to think my singing ability may just land me a record deal if I nailed this cassette tape self-recording of Meredith Edwards' "A Rose Is A Rose," a criminally underrated song I must add.

Confidence has kept me from having severe back troubles (no slouching here) and it has led me to some educational and professional achievements I'm proud of. Confidence also convinced me to move into my first college dorm with a shiny bright pink comforter that resembled plastic Easter grass. I didn't care if I was giving off Elle Woods vibes, I loved that comforter.

Of course, I have my insecurities though, I'd be the worst if I didn't, and those insecurities tend to rear their awkward teenage heads when my confidence has led me down a new highway of adventure and suddenly I realize I'm behind the wheel with only a learner's permit. As I look around on those highways, things are moving fast all around me and I'm left with my foot tentatively on the gas out of necessity but desperately looking for an off-ramp.

Venturing out to build a writing career was one of those highway insecurity times. After writing publicly for over a year and privately for years before that, I felt confident the passionate love affair I had with the written word was a mostly requited love, and I had been known to deliver some actual LOLs which is always a good feeling. Yet it was difficult not to play the comparison game and get stuck in the feeling that I wasn't good enough; two published books into this business and it's still hard to stay focused on my own lane or stop making accidental driving metaphors. These feelings of comparison and self-doubt exist in any career and any business, so much so that they have been studied and given a scientific name - impostor syndrome.

Impostor syndrome is essentially the sinking feeling that you don't deserve to be there. "There" being in a certain group, in a job, or in a position of authority. It's that feeling in the back of your mind that tells you "It's adorable that you think you can do this new thing, but you're a total fraud." You may continue to go into that new job every day and do the work in front of you or chase a big dream, but you are just waiting for someone to come in with the hook and say "Silly you...nice try, but you haven't earned this. Make-believe is over." Are you nodding your head in recognition of this feeling? You aren't alone - it's very common!

Even after I started having my writing published and grew a following on my blog, I still found ways to bump into imposter syndrome. It also came roaring back onto the scene when I wanted to expand the funny motherhood content I was writing to include a piece of my professional experience in career services. I knew the career development work I did in my day job could be valuable to moms at transition points in their lives, and I felt like I could teach the career stuff in a way that was relatable and fun to truly help other people who in many ways were a lot like me. I was super nervous about it though because I wondered if anyone would take me seriously. I had over a decade of professional experience, an advanced degree under my belt, and books upon books on the shelf about career development, but I was only in my thirties and my blog had focused almost entirely on making people laugh up until now. Do people take career advice from thirty-somethings who laugh a lot and tell stories about faking labor on trains to get a seat to themselves? (That's a highly effective method by the way.)

As I thought about combining my coaching and writing

experience with my natural personality to make a career out of it, I had this picture in my mind of what other people might expect out of a career coach. That person didn't look like me. She was older and more serious. She wore tailored business suits, had perfectly coiffed hair, and didn't have to google "what are some serious sounding business words?" so that she could finish this sentence by saying "and she was someone who could pull off saying 'let's circle back to the integration of the profit margin.'"

Career coaching was in my full-time job description at one of the top business schools in the world, but was that only because the higher-ups imagined I DID have a tailored business suit hiding in my closet and that I would get my act together with my hair eventually? Without those real adult things, was I grown up enough to do this job and be taken seriously if I ventured out on my own and did it my own way? I thought there was a market for a coach like me, but I was scared to find out if I was wrong.

As a result of these fears, I almost didn't hit publish on my first blog post that incorporated career development into my parenting humor shtick. When I did hit publish I felt sick to my stomach and then I ran away. Literally. I hit publish at 8:00 AM after dropping the kids off at school, and then I ran out the door. Quickly thereafter I turned my "run" into a brisk walk because running is terrible but the point is I had to get outside because I was so worried I had made a huge mistake by putting myself out there. To manage through this mini panic attack, I put Ben Rector's song "Fear"[1] on repeat in my headphones and kept walking until my stomach settled. I needed that song in particular because there's a beautiful lyric in there that is the perfect antidote to imposter syndrome: "I learned to dance with the fear that I've been running from."

Dance with the fear instead of running from it, embrace the fear and keep moving. I love that "believe in yourself" message because it's more nuanced than a simple, "You can do it!" It's saying that it's okay to be scared, but you need to take that fear and swing it around the dance floor instead of hiding in a bathroom when a slow song comes on. Running away from your goals just takes you farther away from them, but when you're dancing you're taking up space and claiming your spot in the world. So that's what I did, I stopped running, first out of winded necessity, and then out of a renewed belief in my ability to make up a brand new dance and convince others to join in. I went back to the computer, fear in hand, and kept typing through my imposter syndrome to get to the other side.

———

"Believe in yourself" is a lesson we teach our children at every turn as we raise them into humans who will take chances, try new things, and hold their heads up high. Self-confidence is also the most important tool in your career development tool belt so "believe in yourself" is a lesson we need to turn back around on ourselves regularly. Would you hire someone for a job, any job, if they were all "I dunno... I'm fine I guess..." with a big shoulder shrug? Hard pass! You want the person who believes in themselves and their abilities and has managed through their imposter syndrome demons. You want the person who knows they know their stuff and is ready to prove it.

That being said, let's get down to brass tacks about building those self-confidence muscles. I can tell you my stories and ask you to dance all I want but I can't force you out onto the floor like an overly aggressive wedding DJ. I can cheerlead you from the sidelines too and self-confidence can be boosted externally, but the very nature of the word highlights that it has to come from within. You're in charge of this one, friend. You're making the rules. So if you're feeling in need of a self-confidence boost to keep your momentum through this journey and want to learn to dance with the fear instead of running from it, I'm going to offer up a couple of strategies proven to work.

The first recommendation comes from Hal Elrod's *The Miracle Morning*, my bathroom sink, and *Saturday Night Live*. Positive affirmations.

In Elrod's book, *The Miracle Morning*[2], he discusses the power of self-affirmations as part of an effective morning routine to set yourself up for success. When I first read this I was all like "Cool, I'll try that with my kids." I didn't even think about going there for myself. Before bedtime, I would ask Jack and Norah to stand with me in front of the bathroom mirror and repeat "I am strong, I am smart, I am kind, I am funny, I am beautiful, I am loved." I want those words to sink in and become so second nature to them that it's a given. While we aren't as consistent with the practice nowadays, I still sometimes hear Jack and Norah talking to themselves saying "You can do this, you are strong!" and that's a big check in the parenting win column!

Like every other lesson in this book, I knew I had to turn this "believe in yourself" practice inward, even though it was way outside of my self-deprecating comfort zone. If I wanted to work through impostor syndrome and get to the other side then doing a little positive self-talk was certainly worth a shot. Plus, it's backed by science! Research has shown that affirmations can reduce stress, make us less resistant to feedback that helps us improve, and help us shake off negative experiences.[3] That's really cool and worth a few minutes of your time!

I started small with affirmations, and stay small with it to this day. I keep a few affirmations in my back pocket and self-medicate with them as needed: "You're a good mom who is doing the best job she knows how for her kids." "You're an entertaining writer who can make people laugh." "You're an effective coach who makes an impact." Each one hits on a specific part of my identity and having those words on an internal looping record player helps them sink in. There's also another affirmation I keep on speed dial that's a little less traditional. "You can do this with humor and heart."

I use this self-affirmation to remind myself why I'm in this coaching and writing business at all and to keep the focus on what matters most. I want to reach people in a way that is driven by helping (the heart part) and relatable and fun because life is serious enough as it is (the humor part). Repeating this little line encourages me to stay true to myself and believe in my abilities to build a business I can stand behind. Since I know it works, if you don't want to go with the *SNL* classic, "I'm good enough, I'm smart enough, and doggone it, people like me" as an affirmation, try something that is a reminder of what you're good at and what's important to you.

By the way, if you're feeling squeamish about sitting in front of a mirror and self-affirming, take your affirmations on a walk or in the car. Experts say that deep breathing, focus, and looking yourself in the eye in the mirror make your affirmations more powerful, but when it comes to affirming myself I have to do these while I'm on the move or it gets real weird real fast. If you and I are alike and staring deep into your own eyes is uncomfortable and not self-confidence inducing I'm not going to force you into that. See, humor and heart!

———

Another way to boost your self-confidence to improve your career prospects is to channel Ursula from *The Little Mermaid*. Most things about Ursula are terrible, but she makes an important point when she's trying to steal Ariel's voice and send her up to the beach to land a man and teach our daughters very questionable lessons. The importance of body language.

Body language shouldn't be the only tool for communication, but it is a vital part of getting your message across, and how effectively you use your body can have a big impact on success. We know that a firm handshake shows strength and that good posture conveys self-assurance. What I find particularly interesting about body language though is that it can also impact how you feel.

Amy Cuddy, a researcher at Harvard University and bestselling author, is well known for her TED Talk on imposter syndrome and power posing.[4] Cuddy's research focuses on the power of body language to impact not just how others see us, but how we see ourselves. In her studies, she learned that our hormones are affected by our body language, which in turn impacts how we feel and how we interact with the world. What she learned is that it's not only that people might think we aren't confident if our bodies are all slouchy, it's that our hormones will start firing off not-confident signals to our bodies when we're slouchy which cause us to act not confident. Makes your mom's "Sit up straight!" reminders seem a little more meaningful, right?

To take the research a step further, Cuddy tested how changing our body language and "power posing" before going into an interview might change the outcome. A power pose is a stance that takes up physical space and establishes dominance. Kind of like a bear on hind legs, or me when I've told the kids it's bedtime for the 14th time that night and I turn into The Beast roaring about the West Wing.

Participants in Cuddy's study adopted either a low power or a high power pose in front of a mirror before a five-minute, high-stress interview. All else being equal, those who adopted the high power pose were ranked significantly higher than their peers, presumably because of the confidence and power they exuded. It wasn't just what they said in the interview, but how they said it and how they carried themselves.

True to form, after diving into Cuddy's research my brain immediately went to "Implement this with the kids!" As the new school year started and Jack and Norah were heading into new classrooms with new teachers, I knew there was going to be a period of transition and they could use a confidence boost. Kids are incredibly resilient and adaptable, but still, change is hard. So I pulled out my inner Cuddy and before we all clambered into the SUV I asked the kids to stand up tall, put their hands over the heads in fists and say "I CAN DO IT!" It's become a ritual. Kisses, I love yous, "I CAN DO ITs!"

Then one day as I was in a morning rush of my own doing, and someone's request for more cereal's doing, I gave my kids kisses and started to run out the door. I turned around to wave and Norah sat up straight on her stool, put her hands up in the air completely unprompted, and said "I CAN DO IT!"

That's right, little one. You totally can. Now I'm just

going to go pump my fists into the air to remind myself that I've got this too and cry tears of joy in the car. No big deal. Enjoy your Cheerios.

Cliff Notes version of this all this: If you aren't feeling confident, if you're feeling like an impostor, then adopt the body language of someone who is confident, and who feels that she belongs. As we convince others of our awesome, we convince ourselves, and eventually, you go from faking it to being it. You've tapped into the unconscious mind with your body language and changed the way you feel about yourself. You go, girl!

———

Do you remember Gloria Estefan singing "Reach" at the opening ceremonies of the 1994 Olympics? Who am I kidding? Of course, you do. Those inspirational lyrics, the Olympic spirit, that outfit. It was everything. You'll have to google it if you don't remember because I don't know how to embed a YouTube video in a book. Thanks for nothing, college.

There's a beautiful "believe in yourself" message behind that song, and so many songs that have come before it and after it. How spot-on was Taylor Swift? If you get thrown off your game then you've got to shake it off, shake it off. Demi Lovato was right too. There's nothing wrong with being confident. And of course, Shakira was correct, my hips definitely don't lie, although maybe that's beside the point. Those songs all speak to us because confidence is so important. We crave it, we strive for it, and we are impressed by those who have it. As parents we want our children to be filled to the brim with it!

That's what I want for you too, and it's what I want for

myself. I know that if I didn't have confidence I'd hang up the writing success dream, the owning a business dream, and that one very cool dream where I eat chocolate chip cookies with Tina Fey and she laughs at my jokes. It would be disappointing to give up that last one, especially.

Believing in yourself comes from a place of accepting and loving yourself for who you are. Your kids love you and believe in you. Your spouse, family, and friends love you and believe in you. None of them can believe in you FOR you though. That's not how this one works. Believe in yourself, my friend, and use whatever tools work for you to get there. Selfishly, I can't wait to see what you do with all that confidence. It's going to be pretty cool.

CHAPTER 15 NOTES

What affirmations will you use to boost your self-confidence?

Write them out below and then use whatever tools are helpful to you to remember them. Sticky notes on the mirror, reminders on your phone, hiring a skywriter - do what works so you keep up the practice!

SLOW DOWN!

*W*hen I was three years old, my parents gave me a Popples Big Wheel as my first bike. It was purple, adorable, and perfect. Do you remember Popples? If not, they were nonsensical rainbow-colored teddy bears that were first a stuffed toy and then a short-lived 1980s TV show. They also made a brief comeback in 2015 on Netflix because everything old becomes new again.

Back in the day, I peddled around on that Popples bike to my heart's content. Later, I graduated to a bike with training wheels and eventually I was off and rolling on a big kid un-training-wheeled two-wheeled bike. Then I got into my tweens and teens and became very preoccupied with how nerdy I might appear while wearing a helmet. Since I wasn't allowed to ride the bike without one, which was the right call - good work, parents - the bike started to collect dust. That was fine though. I mean, "it's just like riding a bike." If I wanted to get back on the bike, I could do it.

Fast forward twenty years from my last successful bike ride, and Glen and I started dating. He was, and is, athletic and outdoorsy, plus he has calves that just won't quit built over years of soccer, bike riding, and weight training. (He's going to make me take that line out if he carefully reads this chapter, so basically, this is a test of our marriage and how much he supports my dreams. Hi, honey.)

In the first year we were dating, Mr. Bicycle Calves invited me to join him on a bike ride to which the lapsed athlete in me replied, "Oh shucks, I don't have a bike. Guess that conversation is over!" Unfortunately, Glen quickly replied, "Oh it's okay, I have two!"

Of course, you have two bikes...

I decided to be a good sport about it and distinctly remember thinking, "It's just like riding a bike..." but there was a nagging feeling in the back of my mind. It had been two decades since my last ride on a bike that wasn't bolted to the ground. Could I honestly still do this? When I finally got myself onto the bike somehow, I immediately started careening down the hill Glen lived on at the time with no recall of how to stop. I started pedaling backward, but that's not how you slow down a bike, turns out. I screamed at Glen, "I don't know how to stop!!!!!!" and he screamed "Use the brakes, you're a full-grown adult!" and I screamed, "If I knew where the brakes were we wouldn't be having this conversation!!!"

I figured out that bikes have hand brakes before flying into a street that in my memory was akin to the Indy 500 racetrack but in reality was a quiet suburban dead end. For whatever reason we still went on a bike ride that day, but not without incident. I couldn't get the bike going again every time we had to stop at a crosswalk. I forgot where the brakes were again one time and tried to stop the bike with my feet... It wasn't pretty, and perhaps one of the key reasons Glen and I remain happily married to this day is that he never asked me to go on a bike ride again.

Fast forward another ten years, and much like Glen's bachelor pad apartment ten years ago, our house also sits on a little suburban hill. There is very little traffic on our road, but it's still a look-both-ways situation so when we get the kids out on their bikes I need to remind them to slow down on the hill to protect their safety and my blood pressure. These kids are half Calves half me after all and I don't trust my DNA on wheels or hills.

Fortunately they have heeded my warnings for the most part, except for the one time Jack started going way faster than Glen could run and my little guy understandably started to freak out. I had Norah with me and couldn't leave her in the middle of the road, so my contribution to this situation was to scream at Jack "SLOW DOWN!" and then scream at Glen "GO FASTER!" It was confusing for everyone. Eventually, Jack did slow down by ruining a brand new pair of sneakers and Glen tapped into some college athlete speed to catch the bike. No harm, no foul but I may or may not still have nightmares about it. Sneakers are expensive.

How does this bike riding business come back to you and your career? Well, that afternoon bike ride and my prior experience gliding into traffic on two wheels are a good reminder about how we should approach our career development when we're busy trying to move forward faster and faster. This section of the book is all about keeping momentum as you build a career and life you love. We've covered how to do that by getting support, tapping into your bravery, and believing in yourself, but I think another way to keep momentum is to slow down. Maybe even slam on the brakes and come to a hard stop. The fact of the matter is, you've got a lot going on as a mom, an employee/business owner, and a human and if you don't slow down once in a while, life is going to put your car in park for you. I learned this lesson the hard way.

———

It was November 2018, and Glen, Jack, Norah, and I had just spent six days with family in Colorado. We were on the go a lot playing with cousins and exploring parks, malls, and the aquarium, but I also took a lot of tandem naps with Norah that week. It helped her to fall asleep in an unfamiliar location and it helped me to unplug for a little while instead of being in the naptime sprint to accomplish all the things. We also all went to bed at 8:00 PM because it was simply easier to get everyone to sleep in the same room if we called it a day together. I was, in a word, refreshed.

Then we got on an airplane, full of recycled air and germs. and headed back into our regular lives. Within a day of getting back to the east coast I was hacking up a lung and so was Jack. It was just a cold though, so we carried on. I also had a lot to catch up on with work in the office after taking some time off, my blog needed updating, I had book chapters to finish, and I had just started working on brainstorming illustrations for *Belinda Baloney Changes Her Mind*. Oh, and it was the Christmas season, that beautiful time when moms and dads everywhere whip the family into a frenzy of magic. A lot was going on, I had two small needy children, and going to bed at 8:00 PM and taking midday naps was no longer an option back in the real world.

By midweek our house was decked out in Christmas décor and I was deep into online holiday shopping. With a $20 coupon on the counter that was going to expire momentarily, I stayed up late one night to finish creating a photo calendar gift I was working on. I didn't feel well, and I could have used some sleep, but I stayed up to finish the job. Of course the next day I woke up feverish and coughing, but I figured I could make it through the day at work, and that I could still get up super early to bang out a book chapter. At the office, my team needed me there as we were going through a big period of transition, plus I had several meetings on the docket for the day. If I wanted to keep momentum with the big goals I had set for myself and create a new career focused on writing and coaching, then I needed to show up for my day job and get my work done efficiently. That way I'd have time for the other stuff I loved.

In theory, getting yourself motivated to put forth your best effort even when you aren't feeling it seems like a good idea. Mind over matter, do hard things! In reality, it could not have been dumber. Within a half-hour of being in the office my fever spiked up higher and I was dizzy and disoriented trying to lead a meeting. I had to excuse myself twice to lay down on my office floor.

I decided to call it a day by 10:30 AM and stumbled out to the parking lot with tears streaming down my face wondering how I was going to drive myself the 26 miles home. I knew I had to get there and go to sleep though, so my options seemed limited. Fortunately, my boss happened to call my cell phone as I was walking to the car and she immediately recognized that I was quite unwell and should not be responsible for operating a motor vehicle. Another coworker came running out to the parking lot, promptly took my keys, and brought me to the medical center on campus. The nurses there took one look at me and called the ambulance.

Next thing I knew I was in the back of an ambulance, sirens blaring, and hooked up to a half dozen machines. The rest of the story isn't all that exciting because my vitals were fine, I simply had some flu-like symptoms and needed to sleep for a million hours and rehydrate my body. That's exactly the point though: sleep and water. The very basics of human survival were apparently things I was too busy and important to partake in. I desperately needed to slow down and since I wouldn't do that for myself, my body took control and I was bedridden for the rest of the week. I couldn't keep my eyes open long enough to read an email, forget trying to write a chapter for this book. I was physically incapable of leading a meeting or Christmas present wrapping or keeping down my cookies let alone baking a few dozen for neighbors. Everything that had been so important and urgent a few days prior was going to have to wait, and so it did.

———

How about you? How fast are you going right now? You're reading a book, so that's a good start. It hopefully means you are stationary for the time being. But as you are reading this book do you also have a load of laundry in, the dishwasher running, your phone on your lap to check your email, and a dozen other projects running through your mind? Are you plotting out your next big move, mentally refining your goals, realizing it is super late and you need to get to sleep, and then setting your alarm for Very Early O'Clock to have some alone time to focus on your career plan?

There's nothing wrong with those things. There is a lot right with a lot of those things and I'm all for making a plan, setting time for yourself, and being innovative about your career. You are taking charge of where your career goes next and being intentional about achieving your goals. Yet sometimes it all gets to be too much and you need to pump the brakes, and I mean really pump them, not scream at your husband that you don't know how to stop this speeding bike. Take control, slow down, and prioritize what really needs to happen right now and table what can wait.

Finishing this book was a major career goal for me. I had put it out into the ether that I would have the first draft finished by the end of 2018. But you know what, it's early January 2019 as I type this chapter, and I haven't opened this Word document in two weeks. After my little hospital visit, my bad cold never really got better and I ended up with bronchitis and strep throat. In response, I took sick days from work and everyone survived. I went to bed early and stopped setting my alarm, knowing full well that my kids would wake me up before the sun anyway. I drank more water and watched more TV. The book was still here when I came back after Christmas. Work was still going to be there when the university reopened from the winter break. Coaching clients didn't need an answer within four hours, 24 hours was fine. I embraced a couple of weeks of good enough and it was exactly that, good enough.

Being a mom is hard. Being a professional is hard. Trying to figure it all out so we can have it all is hard. Then it only gets harder when we don't recognize that spinning our wheels is sending us deeper into the mud pit instead of propelling us forward. It may seem counterintuitive, but to keep your momentum you need to take a deep breath and stop what you're doing. Unless you are a heart surgeon, then I strongly encourage you to ignore my advice and please continue with the heart surgery because that's super important. Everyone else though, the work is going to still be there if you give yourself a little time away. Your goals aren't going to implode and scatter off into the universe. Instead, you're going to do a better job going after those goals if you get some sleep and recharge those batteries..

And dear heart surgeon, you should go sleep when that surgery is done too. You've earned it!

————

Really struggling to slow down? If that story about the mobile EKG doesn't send you straight to bed, then let's go back to the bikes.

As Jack learned to master the two-wheeler, he had the training wheels still attached. They helped with his balance and confidence and saved us a lot of money on Band-Aids. The training wheels also came in handy when Jack decided to hop in the stroller with Norah one day and I took it upon myself to try his bike. Glen had ridden Jack's little bike before and come on, this thing had training wheels, I'd be fine!

After uttering these famous last words, my dad, who had joined us for the walk, gave me a little push to get going on the bike. Suddenly I was four years old again and I completely forgot everything I had just been teaching Jack about how to stop. As a result, I nearly steered myself off a rather large cliff because I couldn't slow down, again... This time I learned my lesson though, I traded speed for safety and walked the rest of the way home. I got there a little slower as I pushed the bike, and I nicked up my shins as they hit the training wheels, but I didn't crash. By not crashing, I was able to be there for my family and cook a gourmet dinner of hot dogs and baked beans. What would they do without me? I don't even want to think about it.

By taking it slow, I also kept my typing fingers from being broken and my coaching brain from getting knocked around which brought me closer to reaching my goals of creating my own business doing this work. Is it a stretch to say that choosing to get off the bike that day helped me get where I am today? Maybe. However, the moral of the story is that the tortoise can still win the race by taking it slow and steady, and you can too.

CHAPTER 16 NOTES

Remember the essentials:

- Get enough sleep
- Drink water
- Slow down

That's it - that's the whole checklist!

PART V

LET'S TALK LOGISTICS

Time to get down to brass tacks to make money and make moves in your career.

MONEY DOESN'T GROW ON TREES

*J*ack and Norah each have piggy banks on their bookshelves. Jack's is an elephant and Norah has the classic pink pig. They are filled with different coins, and fewer different kinds of bills, courtesy of generous grandparents. The money they save in their piggy banks is usually reserved for trips to Target to pick out a toy and it's also sometimes donated to good causes because these children have hearts of gold. The kids also like to dump all of their money out on the floor to put pennies in rows, learn the names of different coins, or to question if we were trying to pull the wool over their eyes when we gave them an old arcade token as a bribe once.

This coin game is a lot more fun and educational now that Norah is past the young toddler putting everything in her mouth stage; I can't tell you how many pennies I successfully swatted away from her in the early days. Helicopter parenting gets a bad rap, but it's a strategy I'll defend strongly when it comes to toddlers and small objects. We don't have unlimited funds to spend on Emergency Room visits. Money doesn't grow on trees.

I'm bringing this up now because it's time we talk about the elephant in the room, of both the proverbial variety and the ceramic one on Jack's shelf. Money. To be honest with you, if I could have written the whole book without having to talk about money I might have. Not because it's not essential, but because for me, numbers are hard. Really hard, and really dull. Glen tried talking to me about a book he was reading about finance for non-financial managers and I nearly fell asleep standing up. During college, I took an accounting class and would often be found hollering down the hallways, "How did I lose $15,000 on this balance sheet??? I don't understand!"

Money is also a topic that is a bit less comfortable to write on than giving yourself permission to explore new hobbies or talking about your feelings. We can't moonwalk past this one though, we need to talk about money in a career book, because as our parents taught us, and their parents taught them, and like we teach our children as they ogle that fire truck in the store that is an inexplicable $85, things cost money. We don't own the electric company, and, unfortunately, we're not getting our money for nothing or our tips for free.

———

The basic reason we have jobs is so that we can make money and buy the things that we need to survive. I can harp all I want about mental and emotional fulfillment of work, but if your basic human needs are not being met and you don't have food, water, and shelter, then all of this is for naught. Money isn't the key to all happiness, but you, I, and the grocery bills all know that money is something very important.

With that out there on the table and knowing that you need to make money from your career, how much money do you need? When I was making a run to the Dollar Store with piggy bank money as a kid, that answer was clear. As an adult, it gets murkier. A lot of people might answer this by saying "I need to win the lottery!" or throwing a salary number out that is a bit higher than their current salary. That's the easy way out of the conversation. Instead what I'm asking about is your necessity number, which is how much money you and your family need to cover your expenses and save for the future.

For example, if you're saving for a house, what kind of down payment will you need and what will the monthly mortgage be? Do you need a car? What kind of car? How much is your grocery bill, what's your entertainment budget, how many times a year do you want to go visit Grandma? To get started and figure out your own family's necessity number, you need an Excel spreadsheet and you need it stat. Even if you find crunching the numbers painful like I do, this is a particularly important exercise to go through before you dive headfirst into a new job search or explore an entrepreneurial path. Eventually, after you've done all of your career visioning and researching and applying, you are going to be sitting with a job offer in hand that has a number at the bottom. You'll need to know if that number meets your needs or not.

I think about the necessity number like ketchup. I give my kids the ketchup bottle so that they can "do it themselves!" and watch to see what happens. If they put an ocean of ketchup on their plates I tell them that it's too much. If they put a dot, I tell them they might want to put on a little more. (Just kidding, my kids have never put a dot of ketchup on their plates. They always want the ocean.) But if they do the right amount, the amount they know is enough for their nuggets, then that's perfect. This isn't a spot-on analogy, because they can't save away some of their ketchup for their chicken nugget's college fund, but you get it. There's a right amount that meets your needs, and it's generally not ALL the ketchup.

When you take a good hard look at your budget and figure out what your financial needs are, suddenly you have more clarity into what kind of flexibility you have, or don't have right now, to pursue a new path. Could you afford a pay cut if that's what it took to start from scratch in a new industry? What expenses do you have right now that you won't have in two years? Or, are there new expenses on the horizon? Would adjusting your budget right now make a difference for your family?

As I mapped out my future state of an entrepreneurial path, I knew that my current expenses, the necessities, required a stable income, but there was a light at the end of the tunnel when we switched over from daycare to public school. I considered that future expense cut when thinking about how much money I needed to make annually.

There were also some expenses we had right now that weren't necessary and had to hit the cutting room floor. That meant cutting cable TV out of the budget because we had a DVR filled with old episodes of *The Bachelor* from 2013 that I didn't have time for anyway. This netted out to a savings of $75 a month. The budget cuts also meant finding a low-cost grocery delivery service that let me shop online instead of impulse buying random fruit that was going to rot in the crisper or bribe buying my hangry children Cinnamon Toast Crunch so that they would stay in the cart. There's a cost associated with grocery delivery, but at the end of the day, the change saved me time and money. Taking a look at your habits and trying something new can make a big difference for your bottom line, and a new bottom line gives you more freedom to explore a new path and take a (very literally) calculated risk.

When you hit the end of this chapter, get your personal finance guru hat on and start thinking about your salary needs. Write down your goals, write down your expenses, and get to work on that spreadsheet. This doesn't have to be super complicated to ballpark where you need to be money-wise. If you're struggling with it though, grab the ear of a professional since when filling out their career and life criteria, financial advisors wrote down things like "I love crunching numbers and helping people." Seems like a cool person to know right about now, eh?

———

Sometimes I wonder if my children will grow up to work in the finance sector because they are great with addition, and even better with subtraction. "He took one of my crackers! Now I have fewer crackers than him! Oh, the humanity!" Another fitting path forward would be car salespeople because their negotiation skills are on point. How did we end up having two desserts tonight? Because Jack asked for three and somehow this is the compromise we ended up with. Played me like a fiddle...

Speaking of negotiation, you might have thought that since this chapter was about money, this book is geared towards moms, and I'm a female career coach I was going to be spending the whole time shouting from the rooftops, "Women don't negotiate! Know your worth!" That is 100% true, and we'll get there, but first I have to say that the tendency not to ask for more is not so deeply ingrained that we can't shake it as women. I've seen Norah negotiate her way up to sleeping with fifteen stuffed animals when my original offer was three... Women can ask for, and get, more, but it's not as simple as just asking nicely. There are stats and strategies behind this. Numbers behind the numbers, if you will.

First things first, the gender wage gap that we talked about earlier. As of 2020, white women were making 81 cents for every dollar a man makes and the wage gap figure goes down to 75 cents to the dollar for Hispanic and Black women.[1] This pay gap impacts day to day spending power, long term savings, retirement, and decisions around child-care. Remember our chat about 2020? While I never in a million years expected to be typing this when I first started writing this book in 2018, 860,000 US women dropped out of the workforce in September 2020 due to childcare needs.[2] Someone had to do it and families looked at their income and made tough choices. For many, that meant women making lower salaries took a step back and men stayed at work.

Now let's get down to why the gender wage gap exists and how this ties into negotiation. First, one of the reasons the wage gap exists is because of what is known as "the motherhood penalty." I kid you not, that's an actual term. Basically what this means is that women get paid less because they are more likely to take a career break to stay home with children and their resume gap impacts "qualifications" for higher-paying roles. It also means that women experience discrimination at work because it is assumed that they will step out of the workforce when they become mothers and therefore shouldn't be given increased responsibilities or promotions. I wish I was making this up, and I doubly wish that people will get it together enough to ditch their biases by the time my children are hitting the work-force. Both of my children currently say that they want to be parents someday, but that's only going to negatively impact Norah's career, even if she decides she's on the fence about having children? Nope. Big old nope to that.

Another reason for the gender wage gap is the differences between which careers women and men enter. Take a look at the highest-paying jobs in the US and many of these roles are STEM-related and based on academic areas young girls have historically been pushed away from. That bias doesn't just upset the gender balance in a classroom, it has long term effects on earnings. Yet, even if women and men are doing the exact same job, and have the exact same qualifications, women are still paid less. That's where the argument tends to go, right? Women and men are doing different work so it makes sense they are paid differently? It's just not true though. Even for the same work, women are paid 98 cents to the dollar as compared to men.

To put this in lemonade stand terms, that would mean even if Jack and Norah put together the lemonade stand together, spent equal time mixing the lemonade, and were equally good at selling lemonade, customers would give Norah two cents less because she's a girl. To quote the great Stepanie Tanner, "How rude!"

Clearly, there are societal issues we need to break down to address the gender wage gap, and we should do that important work together. There is a piece of this that is in our control in the short term as individuals though and that comes back to our discussion on negotiation. Studies have shown that women are less likely to ask for higher salaries in offer negotiations for new jobs or in their current roles, and since they don't ask they don't receive them. Then when you start from a lower salary, it is going to take longer for that salary to increase. The simple takeaway on this one - you need to ask! To do that, reread the chapter about believing in yourself to boost your confidence, and then follow these steps:

Step one: Know your salary needs. We've covered that in our talk about budgeting and expenses.

Step two: Do your research. Websites like Salary.com, Glassdoor, and Indeed give some insight into expected salaries at positions so you can do some benchmarking. You can even do searches based on industry, location, and function.

Step three: If this is a new position for you, consider all of the elements of the job offer and what is most meaningful to you, from financial, professional, and personal perspectives. Write them down, rank order them, and think about what specifically you want to ask for, financially or otherwise.

Step four: Give yourself a big old affirmation filled pep talk because we're going in to talk turkey.

When I was in the position to negotiate early on in my career, I did step four but not steps one through three. I simply looked at two job offers, saw one with a higher salary, and geared up the nerve to ask the other organization to match it. They didn't, and I took the job anyway.

Fast-forward nine years and I had gained some of that important knowledge. I looked at my salary in late 2016 and found that my bank account was getting dangerously low. The biggest impact - double daycare bills for a baby and a toddler. Yikes. My take-home pay was less than what I was paying weekly for daycare and that was not working. More specifically, it made me want to cry in the shower a lot. Then I crunched the numbers some more based on publicly available salary information and found my salary was well below the median for my tenure and the contributions I made to the team. I valued the flexibility of my job and the people I worked with, but I also valued my worth and ability to go to work without feeling like I was costing my family money.

Armed with all of that information, plus a "go get 'em, girl" pep talk, I laid out my case for my manager based on facts, including details about my financial obligations. It was a good case, and my manager agreed. Her boss agreed. Human Resources agreed. It didn't happen the next day, but eventually, my salary was bumped up and I hardly rocked the boat. None of this would have happened if I hadn't asked. Sure, Human Resources reviews salaries, but no one is going to care quite as much about your financial well-being as you do, except maybe your spouse or partner. So go ahead and ask for what you feel you deserve with the confidence of a two-year-old who negotiates for a snack shortly after not eating her dinner. Just make sure you do so with your ducks in a row, and as the reasonable and respectful person you are. If it goes well, awesome. You're a rock star. If you don't get the outcome you hoped for, you are still a rock star. You asked, and you'll be prepared to take it on again in the future.

———

Here's the thing about money we haven't mentioned. Some of you reading may be in a position in which you are currently unemployed and need to be employed. Maybe you took time out of the workforce and now your financial situation has changed and you need to bring in more income immediately. Maybe there were layoffs at your job, your savings are dwindling, and you need to find a way to support your family ASAP.

For everyone in this boat, I strongly encourage you to use all of the advice here about uncovering where your career sweet spot lies, finding themes within the work you have enjoyed, and using your words to help get what you really want. At the same time, I fully appreciate that you need to find a job to pay the bills now. Yesterday perhaps. So let's do exactly that with some very tactical advice found in the chapters that will follow. With these job search tools and money-making strategies, you'll work yourself into a more comfortable financial situation and then you can keep doing the activities that you know will help you get to a better place like building your network, getting creative, and learning new skills. Even if money did grow on trees, much to my children's displeasure, trees do not grow overnight, and there are steps to this process that may include a job you aren't crazy about but helps you get where you need to go.

There are other things that didn't happen overnight either that I'll be dealing with shortly when these children wake up. For example, it is not Christmas morning yet, it isn't snowing, it is not the weekend, and we're out of apple juice. Oh, and Amazon didn't bring the new Spiderman pajamas yet. Things about to get rough up in here... Wish me luck.

CHAPTER 17 NOTES

Sample Budget Sheet

Your income and expenses may look very different, but you can use this as a jumping off point.

Monthly Income			Monthly Savings	
Primary Income - You	$		~20% of monthly income	$
Primary Income - Partner	$			
Additional Income 1	$		**Monthly Expenses**	
Additional Income 2	$		Housing	$
TOTAL	$		Utilities	$
			Groceries	$
			Transporation	$
			Education	$
			Childcare	$
			Medical	$
			Debt Repayment	$
			Extracurricular Activities	$
			Entertainment	$
			Clothing	$
			Other	$
			TOTAL	$

4 Steps of Negotation

- Step 1: Know your salary needs.
- Step 2: Do your research.
- Step 3: Consider all of the elements of the job offer and what is most meaningful to you, from financial, professional, and personal perspectives. Write them down, rank order them, and think about what specifically you want to ask for, financially or otherwise.
- Step 4: Affirmation filled pep talk!

NO ONE GOES TO THE CIRCUS TO SEE A ONE BALL JUGGLER

*A*s a teenager, I spent a lot of time juggling. I sincerely wish I meant real juggling because that would have made me a much more interesting person. Instead, I mean juggling school work, soccer practice, softball practice, basketball practice, piano, student club leadership, memorizing *NSYNC lyrics, and AOL instant messenger. There was also the one season in which on top of all of that I spent several weeks preparing for a beauty pageant scholarship program and brushing up on my performance sign language. (I wasn't that great at the piano and I needed a talent for the pageant. I also wasn't that great at performance sign language, as it turned out, which is one of several reasons why you didn't see Miss America listed on my list of past jobs.)

As the 90s became the 00s I was also focusing on college applications, which can be pretty stressful, especially for a kid who had essentially tattooed "perfectionist" on her face but wouldn't actually get a tattoo for fear of how it might impact her college applications. I felt a lot of pressure riding on this decision and my anxiety kicked into high gear as the now-familiar stress bubbles started to build up in my chest. How was I going to do all of the things I had signed up to do while at the same time thinking about my future? It was then that my dad gave me some of the best tough love I've ever received and uttered a piece of advice that's become a famous Pop-ism for its bluntness, realism, and suck-it-up-sweetheartness: "No one goes to the circus to see a one-ball juggler."

Soak that one in. It's completely true. Would you pay $19.99 to see a dude in the middle of a circus tent throwing one single ball up and down? No, you're paying for at least three balls, maybe a sword, ideally something is on fire, and that juggler is balancing on a beach ball on a tightrope. Now that's worth the price of admission. I'd tell my friends about that juggler. If successful, that juggler would be getting a very nice Yelp review.

The point behind his statement was clear. True, you have a lot on your plate, and yes, you could really push to excel at one single thing and you could be comfortable in that thing and even make a living at that thing. However, there is value in having a few different balls in the air. The diversification of your life makes it more interesting for you, but also for the people around you. It also provides a safety net so that you have fallback plans should one ball drop. When I throw this theory up against a wall to see if it sticks, my mind goes right to Lady Gaga. She busted onto the scene as a circus of one, but then look at how she has evolved and kept multiple balls in the air. Her songwriting, her dancing, her costume choices, her connection with fans, her comedy chops, her acting... That's a lot of juggling, and we are paying the price of admission.

Pop's point wasn't to drive yourself to the point of exhaustion to bring in an audience or make a living. He was simply saying keeping multiple balls in the air is impressive, interesting, and a potential path to success. When I look at my life right now, I know with certainty that no one would be going to the circus that is my blog if I wasn't doing some pretty good juggling. There wouldn't be anything to write worth laughing about it if I wasn't managing the chaos of a family with small children, managing my career development while helping others do the same, and managing to find the humor in all of it. I need the juggle to keep the circus going, and while I prefer sweatpants and need my alone time to recharge my batteries, I also really like an audience. A digital audience, who is also in sweatpants.

This would be the point in the chapter where I would bring in an example of how I have used this parenting technique with my kids and have taught them the value of diversifying your life. However, they are barely out of Pull-Ups and I appreciate their singular focus on getting their oatmeal into their mouths successfully instead of all over the dining room floor. Therefore, it's probably best that we wait on this parenting gem for a few years but I'm sure I'll find myself saying it at some point when I'm channeling my parents' ability to break up a pity party.

————

This whole juggling business does have a very obvious connection to parenthood though. Motherhood in particular. Moms are the ultimate jugglers. Masters of the juggle. Juggler extraordinaires! Think about everything you are doing on a daily basis. Keeping children fed, clothed, and safe. Keeping yourself fed, clothed, and safe. Driving to school drop-off, and swim class, and doctor's appointments. For some, managing a full-time job outside of your home.

For others, volunteering, helping your neighbors, or managing your work from anywhere business. Maybe all of these things! You are trying to get enough sleep, exercise, and practice the self-care every magazine is telling you is important. You're also reading a book, like right now! You are a freaking magician. I will absolutely pay to see your juggling act.

Now I'm asking you to throw another ball into the air because I'm a terrible, horrible person who knows your potential. That ball is your career development and while it can feel like a burden to keep this ball/flaming baton/piano up in the air, it's so worth it.

When I started getting serious about finding more fulfillment and joy in my career, I came to realize that even though there are only so many hours in a day, 24 hours is a lot of hours and I could find ways to toss this ball into the act if I got creative. It was up to me to use the hours I had so that I didn't stay stuck in the rut of saying "But there's not enough time" like a broken record. That song has been played out and no one wants to hear it no matter how true it might feel for you. (I'm not great at tough love - was that too harsh? Are you okay? I love you and I'm proud of you!)

The first step to taking back my time was figuring out which balls I could put down or at least hand over to a partner so I could get a breather. That started with getting better at dividing and conquering at home, which I know isn't an option for everyone but it's something I recommend if possible because as women we tend not to do this enough. I wasn't the only one who could cook dinner during the week, so Glen and I figured out a better system to split up the work. Same thing with answering emails from the kids' school or planning birthday parties. Some of this stuff needed to be split up more, and I needed to give up control so that I could use a little bit of time outside of work to figure out what I wanted and how to get there. It's amazing how those minutes add up to hours of productivity, and it was cool to see what I could do with suddenly free moments. Even if splitting up the household work simply meant that I could go take a stress-free shower, that helped! Remember, quiet time is huge for tapping into your creativity and problem-solving. Plus, showers are nice, I might go take one right now...

Then I turned to the hours between 9 and 5 and thought about how I was using that time. I couldn't wave a magic wand and make the days longer so I could spend more time coaching or writing during my day job, but I figured out what things I could do more efficiently, how early I would be willing to get up in the morning to handle my to-do list, and what activities I was supposed to have delegated years ago but held onto because again, control issues. For example, this meant trusting my team to manage their projects without me looking over their shoulder, using technology to automate emails that took forever to send, learning some new tricks in Excel to make data processing easier, and yes, getting up way before the sun to write.

With all that, I put some balls down, handed over others, and threw some balls extra high up in the air to create more room in my daily schedule at the office to shadow other career coaches and take on writing projects. I proved to myself and my bosses that I could juggle cooler more interesting balls not by dropping others but by keeping up the ones that mattered and gently placing others on the shelf.

———

I know what you're going to say and you're right. Just like "divide and conquer" isn't always an option, the "change up the 9-5" strategy to pivot your career doesn't work for everyone either. Perhaps at the office you can jump on another task force or learn a new skill, but your manager isn't supportive of you making a change. Or your job is very structured and there simply isn't space to do less or add more, at least not during work hours. Every situation is different and again the magic wand would be nice right now, but I did not get into Hogwarts.

Sans magic though, you can still work the juggling act, take your career in a new direction, and make some more money by adding in a side hustle. Don't run away because I used the term side hustle! Please! There's a really good cookie recipe embedded in here as a reward for sticking through my side hustle pep talk, plus I'm going to convince you that side hustles are both awesome and worth it. Deep breath and...go!

Beyond being a side hustler myself as you've heard about throughout this book, I've listened to enough of the *How I Built This* podcast on NPR to know that I'm far from the only one who has chased a dream on the side before making it my full-time gig. Most often the step before running a full-time business is a side hustle because realistically we all need income to pay our bills and stable steady already existing jobs are the safest way to do that. Therefore, before most entrepreneurs go out on their own, they work on their idea on the side, hustle at it, if you will, and start bringing in a little bit of money while keeping the lights on with other sources of income.

Remember the book *Eat, Pray, Love* by Elizabeth Gilbert? Of course, you do, it's that book turned Julia Roberts movie about self-discovery that sent everyone and their mom off to Italy, or at least to the Olive Garden for some guilt-free pasta. Gilbert had written several books before her major bestseller and writing was her side hustle the whole time because as she says in her book, *Big Magic*,[1] she didn't want her creativity to be responsible for her livelihood. Turns out it could be which was awesome, but she was happy hustling until she got there because she loved the work.

There are dozens of more examples of side hustles turned into full-time jobs and massive companies; Instagram started as a side hustle, Apple was a side hustle, Mattel was a side hustle, Harley Davidson was a side hustle! If the entrepreneurial life is for you, I don't need to spend much more time convincing you about the power of adding a side hustle ball into your juggling act. It's the clear and least risky path forward for starting a business.

You don't need to want to be a full-time business owner though for this side hustle stuff to be worthwhile. My path doesn't have to be your exact path, it would almost be weird if it was because we're all different with unique career and life criteria guiding our choices. Still though, if you're feeling stuck in your career and want to try something new, a side hustle can help you do that without leaving your job or it can fill the gaps if you're unemployed.

I know teachers who make and sell door signs, lawyers who do freelance writing, stay-at-home moms who have Etsy shops filled with educational materials, and bankers who bake. Their passion projects aren't their full-time gigs right now, and for many of them, entrepreneurial life wouldn't be the right fit so that's not the goal. The goal is to tap into their curiosity and unique skills so that they feel fulfilled in their careers and lives. The extra money it brings in doesn't hurt either because these folks are parents responsible for buying snacks on snacks on snacks.

People make money in all kinds of ways using their hands, their brains, and their hearts. If you feel something stirring just below the surface that you want to try, try it. Unless that stirring is calling you to own a giraffe sanctuary, the upfront costs of pursuing a passion as a hobby or side hustle are pretty low. Cut your expenses a bit and you've found your wiggle room to invest in yourself. Then you can start building something you love, maybe bringing those skills back to your 9-5 or maybe not, all the while maintaining the financial stability your family needs.

The resume coach in me has to chime in here too because side hustles can be amazing resume builders. We're going to dive into resumes, cover letters, and career storytelling in the next chapter, but for now let me say that if you have worked on something outside of your full-time job, that can and should go on your resume. You can and should talk about it in interviews too. It's completely appropriate to talk about the different skills you have and the businesses you've been able to build as part of your career story. No one has to give you the job you want to be able to include it on your resume, you can create it for yourself! It's a lot of work to juggle a side hustle, but it also opens doors to possibilities and a ton of personal fulfillment, as long as you're not trying to juggle grand pianos. If that's the case, put one of those pianos down. You're going to hurt your back.

Speaking of heavy things, there's yet another elephant in the room we haven't talked about - Multi-Level Marketing companies (MLMs) and the high school acquaintances sending friend requests on social media and then immediately pitching night cream in your DMs. That's the snarky take on this, and in many cases, it's not far from the truth as we've all seen and experienced. It's also the reason "side hustle" can get a bad rap.

There's a big "But" coming though. I turned the corner on being more supportive of the MLM side hustle when I saw people I knew and liked genuinely enjoying the process. The realization that someone involved in a MLM might be doing so because they have another job that isn't completely fulfilling something in their life or a financial need that wasn't being met was like a smack to the career coach head. The folks who join MLMs could be doing so to see if sales could be an ideal career path for them, or they might have an interest in the beauty industry they want to explore further. Whatever it is, people choose to get involved in these businesses for valid reasons and I'm all for experimenting in your career to see what works and what doesn't. I have some questions about the MLM business structure and tactics, but not the motivation or the potential upside for professional growth. Side hustle on, friends!

For a list of 55 side hustles, see the notes page at the end of this chapter and read more about them on withlovebecca.com. The world is full of potential, you just need to tap into yours!

(Oh, and I promised a cookie recipe for sticking with me here. Check out the back of the Tollhouse Chocolate Chip bag as your starting point, but instead of two sticks of butter do one and ⅞ sticks of margarine. Then sub the two eggs for half a cup of plain greek yogurt. Lastly, add half a bag of chocolate chips and half a bag of butterscotch chips to the dough. You're welcome.)

———

Adding in more work to a plate that already feels full can seem impossible. Yet if it was impossible then how do people do it every day? How do they maintain a stable career, raise their children, and join yet another company or start something new on their own? They do, and they have the same number of hours in the day that you do. Some of those people may have some extra help or some extra money, that's true, but not all of them. A lot of those people have simply learned how to juggle extremely well. Like anything, it takes some practice, and maybe some YouTube tutorials, but it's possible. Plus, once you get better at it, you'll find that you can juggle more, and be excited about juggling more.

In addition to the juggling tactics we've covered so far, here are some more super practical time-saving and productivity suggestions to keep all those balls in the air. To find more time in your day, you could wake up a half-hour before the kids, stop watching Netflix after one episode, outsource something economically (grocery delivery, house cleaning, lawn mowing), or block time on your calendar to do a certain task all in one chunk.

To save yourself more time, you could serve breakfast for dinner, serve leftovers for dinner, serve frozen pizza for dinner! I realize those ideas are very dinner specific, but dinner is a pain in the neck if you let it be. You can also reclaim your time by taking a class that will teach you how to accomplish a task more efficiently, or even as Laura Vanderkam says in her book *168 Hours*[2], you can simply lower your standards. Your entire house does not need to be spotless at all times. Your underwear does not need to be folded. Letting go of some things in favor of time to deal with the big things makes a big difference. Moving on to some multitasking suggestions. Try educational podcasts in the car, audiobooks while you're cooking, reading on the elliptical, or leaving yourself voice memos when you don't have time to write down that great idea. There are lots of options here!

Even one little change from any of these time-saving and productivity categories can help you keep your juggle going, and I know that for certain because I use them all! While writing this book I was also working full-time, maintaining a blog, freelance writing, creating tons of memes because memes are fun, and coaching private clients nights and weekends. I was juggling, and sometimes it was exhausting, but mostly I loved it. Plus through this juggle, I showed my kids how having multiple careers can be really cool and now Jack is considering being a Navy Seal who writes chapter books before pursuing a career as a scientist. That's awesome. Side hustles are great for the money, but that right there, seeing my kids watch me and then dream their own dreams, that's the good stuff.

———

Like moms, kids are expert jugglers too. For example, Norah likes to juggle eating dinner with singing, mid-meal hugs, and tending to her stuffed animals. Jack likes to juggle putting on his shoes with making Tinker Toy swords, that suddenly become fire hoses, and then cannons, and then Nerf guns because Mommy gets all twitchy when he says it's a gun and he knows to add Nerf as a qualifier. Each of my kids bounces from one idea to the next which to be 100% honest, can drive me nuts.

When I think about it though—alone in the dark when these things aren't happening—these two are learning to be creative, juggle different ideas and activities at the same time, and make their lives beautiful and exciting. That's pretty cool and I think it's going to take them places. However, I'm going to need you to remind me about this moment of clarity when I cannot get my kids out the door to school later because one of them is singing into their toothbrush and the other one is reading books in their underwear. Thank you in advance for your help in this matter.

CHAPTER 18 NOTES

Sides Hustle Ideas

Writing
   Blogging
   Freelance Writing
   Write a Book

Audio/Visual
   YouTube Channel
   Social Media Influencer
   Podcasting

Business to Consumer Services
   Coaching
   Resume Writing
   Childcare

Business to Business Services
   Consulting

Bookkeeping
Virtual Assistant
Editing/Proofreading
Transcribing

Technical

Graphic Design
Web Design

Education

Teaching
Online Courses
Selling Printable Worksheets

Transportation/Delivery

Instacart
Uber/Lyft
Amazon
Grubhub

Online Shop

Tshirts
Drinkware
Quilting/Knitting
Jewelry
Pottery

Art

Photography
Greeting Cards
Painting/Drawing
Woodworking

Food

    Baking

    Cooking

    Creating Recipes

Health and Wellness

    Fitness Instruction

    Meal Planning

    Sports Coach

Sales

    Direct Sales

    Retail/Customer Services

    Real Estate

    Yard Sale Sites

    Airbnb

Beauty

    Hair Styling

    Makeup Artist

    Personal Stylist

Animal Care

    Dog Walking

    Pet Sitting

Household

    Cleaning

    Organizing

    Home Decorating

Nature

    Lawn Work

Selling Plants
Plant Care Education

Investing
Stock Market
Real Estate

LET'S READ A STORY

I have loved books my whole life and have passed on this love of the written word to my children. Their bookshelves are filled to the brim with everything from board books to chapter books and I'll happily add more to the collection. Reading Rainbow was 100% correct in my humble opinion; take a look it's always in a book.

However, there are times I regret passing on my book obsession to my children. For instance, when Norah asks to read the Halloween book *Click, Clack, Boo* three times in a row before bed. In July. It's a lovely book, but I can only be surprised that Farmer Brown wins Best Costume so many times. Oh, spoiler alert, sorry. Or when the kids act exactly like childhood me and get distracted by a book when putting on their cleats and we end up 15 minutes late to soccer practice. And if Jack finds that 465-page book about the magical fairies that I hid in my closet then I'm in for it, because I'll be reading to him about fairies until I'm dead. My tombstone will read, "She died doing something she loved, mostly."

For the most part, I'm here for the book love though because there is research upon research showing the power of books for kids. It helps future literacy, brain development, understanding of the world, and imagination. We are taught, and rightly so, to read to our kids. Therefore, when Jack and Norah ask us to read a book or make up a story on the fly, Glen and I almost always oblige. I bet you do too with your kids. You're such a great parent. Has anyone told you that today? Seriously, you're crushing it.

Our brains are wired to be sucked in by stories as adults too. It's why we love Shonda Rhimes and her ability to weave a plot on Thursday nights. It's why we end up sitting on the couch watching the rest of that *Daniel Tiger's Neighborhood* episode after the kids have left the room. Prince Wednesday looked pretty upset about his broken trombone and we need to know what happens next. Stories pull us in and engage our brains in a way that facts, figures, and lists simply don't. Here's another example. Would you be excited to listen to a speech that started like this: "Hi, my name is Linda. I am here to talk to you about the history of copper." Snooooooooooooze. No, thank you. However, even if the topic is something painfully dull, a story livens it up. What if Linda started her talk on the history of copper with this instead?

"Everyone reach into your wallet and find a penny. Look at the back of that penny and find the year. Now try to think hard about a memory you have from that year. It's a part of your history, a part of your life story. The back of my penny says 1903, and that's exactly where I want to start my story. It's not my life story, but the life story of this penny and the story of how your penny ended up in your wallet today."

Even though I just completely made up that speech, I want to go listen to imaginary Linda give her talk now.

Something chemical in my brain clicked on when Linda started telling me the story of a particular penny instead of telling me she was going to teach me about copper.

A big part of your career development is telling your story. Now that you've put in the groundwork to figure out what you want, you're going to need to talk about yourself in a way that makes others turn on their listening ears. You do that by telling a story on paper and in person.

For anyone on the job hunt, that will mean resumes, cover letters, and interviews, but for those wanting to start a business the guiding principles of story we are going to talk about still apply. When I realized I wanted to venture out as an entrepreneur and I started building websites, writing books, preparing for webinars, and attracting new clients, my brain immediately went to story, every time. So, if the resume, cover letter, and interview words make you cringe because you're not a massive career nerd like me, or because you don't see how it applies to you, stick with me. We're going to make this fun!

———

Let's kick things off by writing a standout resume that's going to come in handy for job applications and networking. Once upon a time you probably wrote a resume and included your name, the jobs you've had, and the schools you went to. That's the start of a good resume, but a great resume takes it up a notch and tells your story to a potential employer or new connection. It's a piece of paper that packs a punch and says "I'm exactly the lady you need for this job!" That may not sound like storytelling on the surface, but it is.

You can kick off that story on your resume by introducing yourself with a Professional Profile or Summary. This resume section offers up a written ten-second elevator pitch about why you're awesome and lets you write the first chapter to your story instead of handing over that job to a bunch of company names and dates. To clarify "elevator pitch," imagine this: you're in an elevator with Ms. Manager of your dream job, and you have one floor before she's getting off. What do you say that convinces her to take your resume back with her to her desk? The summary can be an especially helpful section if you are making a career change or re-entering the workforce after some time away because it focuses on the valuable skills you bring to the table.

To show you how this works, my daughter, Norah, is going to apply for the role of "Friday night movie chooser." I must say that Norah's credentials are pretty strong, but she does only have four years of experience compared to her competitors who have five years, 35 years, and 37 years of experience selecting movies. She's going to need to sell it to the employer that she is the right woman for the job. Norah's first pass on her job application included an objective on the top of her resume instead of a summary. If you haven't seen one before, an objective on a resume is a one-liner that says "I want a new job." Kind of like this:

Objective: I WANNA WATCH MOANA. Jack picked last time, Ursula is scary, and also I WANNA SNACK.

Yeah...no. That's not going to work. Try again, Norah.

Objective: To pick the movie we watch on Friday night and to have that movie be Moana.

Okay, that's better, but as Ms. Manager in this situation, Norah's objective didn't give me much more information about why I should pick her for the job. So we did some coaching and I suggested she try a resume summary instead. Something like this:

Summary: Dedicated professional passionate about modern cinema and inspired by the power of film to move an audience. Skilled in proposing unique and effective solutions independently and as part of a team. Committed to promoting strong role models in the media to help build the foundation for future generations to tackle the problems of today and tomorrow.

Now we're talking! Norah introduced the main character of the resume story (her) while highlighting why she would be great at picking the movie. From here she can move on to the rest of her story knowing that as a reader I'm interested to see what's going to happen next. As we move along to the next stage of your Chip and Joanna style resume remodel, keep looking at your resume from the employer's perspective and think about what they see and what story you want them to be reading.

The meat and potatoes of your resume is the Experience section which gives a rundown of what you've been up to career-wise for the past decade or so. Here most people include bullet points from their job descriptions that start like "Responsible for..." or "Worked on..." It's accurate, but it doesn't tell Ms. Manager a whole lot about what you're great at. Instead, let's think about each bullet point under each job as a short story about a skill you've developed that drives results. By using strong action-oriented words and taking credit for your accomplishments, you come across as confident and competent on paper. That's what we want! Here's an example of making the change from "meh" to "yes!" in your resume bullet points.

"Meh" bullet point: Responsible for building new client relationships as part of the sales and marketing strategy.

"Yes!" bullet point: Built new client relationships by prospecting small businesses in the area, understanding their key pain points as they relate to computer software, and offering budget appropriate solutions. New clients led to 20% increase in company revenue in 2017.

Do you see how that's better? It hits on the problem the company faced, the action you took, and the result you drove. You still talked about your previous job, but you told a little story by getting more specific about what you did, how you did it, and the impact your actions made.

One more example for stay-at-home parents going back to work outside the home.

"Meh" bullet point: Responsible for the care of my two children under the age of five.

"Yes!" bullet point: Managed household logistics for my family of four including primary caregiver responsibilities for my two young children under age five. Planned all weekly meals, organized educational activities inside and outside the home, and coordinated health care needs.

You're accomplishing a lot every single day in your job, don't gloss over it with a "just a stay-at-home mom" or skip past the details. There are a lot of details going down in your house and you're in charge of them as a teacher, caregiver, head chef, and patient advocate. Those skills translate perfectly to roles that need multitasking pros who can keep the ship afloat. Let your resume tell your story!

Two more quick points on resumes before we move along. Does the job you're applying for require specific skills (computer skills, communication skills, nunchuck skills)? Think about adding in a Skills section on your resume to make sure it's super clear you have exactly what the employer is looking for. To do this look at the qualifications for your dream job and then match that up with a list of what you're great at, like building relationships, analyzing data, or public speaking. Include what is most relevant.

You can also think about adding in a Personal section that shows an employer that you aren't a one-dimensional worker bee, but a real live person they want to get to know. By showing a bit about your personality, you're adding more layers to your character's story and telling the reader that you're the candidate with great skills who is also interested in photography, learning foreign languages, or soccer—this could make you stand out a bit more. The interviewer on the other side of your resume isn't one-dimensional either and you could have something in common. Or your creative streak, travel experience, or sense of humor could make you an even better candidate for the job. Bonus!

Need a little more resume help? Check out a sample resume at beccacarnahan.com.

———

Now onto the next chapter of our story, cover letters. I've read many cover letters in my day, both as a hiring manager and as a career coach. And of course, as a storyteller and career nerd, I love them. I'm always actively rooting for the cover letter to knock it out of the park and pull me right into the story. While a resume is a great snapshot of your experience, a cover letter highlights your interest in a specific job, shows off your communication style, and most importantly, tells a company why they should hire you to come solve their problems.

When you're writing an email to a potential client as a business owner you should be doing the same thing. You're making a sales pitch, and the product you're selling is either something you made, your skills, or the goods in your brain. Often cover letters and outreach emails don't sell effectively though and they can land in an employer's digital recycling bin quicker than you can holler down the hall "I said stop bothering your sister!" You can fix this though, with a little help from my son, Jack.

Jack loves to push the kid-sized grocery carts when we go to the store. You know, those squeaky-wheeled little things designed to keep kids occupied and nip at your ankles for 45 minutes? To get this coveted job, Jack has to submit a job application and knock the socks off the hiring manager who is quite busy and wants to get this grocery shopping done efficiently, and with minimal chasing of children through the narrow aisles of the wine department.

As part of his job application, Jack wrote a cover letter. Here's his first try.

Cover Letter 1

Mommmmmmmmy, Mommmy, Mommmy, MOM,

I wanna push one of those little grocery carts because it would be so fun for ME! I would have the freedom that sitting in the big cart just does not afford and this would make me happy. Or I want 11 lollipops instead. Please. PLEASEEEEEEEEE. I REALLY want this job.

PLEASE!

Jack

When reading this cover letter, as the hiring manager I was annoyed right off the bat by the casual tone of Jack's request and the poor grammar. Also, while I learned how much this job would benefit Jack as an applicant, I learned nothing about how hiring Jack would serve my company. Not hired. (Or hired begrudgingly because I desperately needed to pick up a gallon of milk and didn't feel like dealing with a tantrum in the dairy aisle.)

With some encouragement, Jack tried rewriting his cover letter.

Cover Letter 2

Dear Ms. Mommy,

The Team Family organization has done excellent work in the areas of staff development, budgeting, and meal planning. I am particularly impressed by the level of care you give each employee, and how opportunities for growth benefit both the individual and the team.

I am excited about the prospect of contributing to your organization in the position of Small Grocery Cart Driver. Given my previous experience in being a big helper, I know I could add value to your team. I have the proven ability to select the perfect bag of baby carrots, find the exact number of yogurts you are looking for, and pick boxes that are very low to the ground. Furthermore, I am a good listener with excellent driving skills, which will help the Team Family organization achieve its goals.

I look forward to speaking with you about this position further. Thank you for your consideration.

Best regards,

Jack

This time around, I learned why Jack was excited about this job and could see how his contributions would help my company. The connection between his skills and my needs as the manager was made super clear. Hired! Or at least called for a first-round phone interview. Let's not get hasty.

Cover letters are a story about you, but it's essential to keep in mind that this isn't a wish list for Santa. You want the role; the employer gets that, but why should they hire you instead of someone else? Put yourself in Ms. Manager's shoes as you're writing and try to understand what she's looking for out of this role. Then as you tell your story, weave in the important things that set you apart and include examples that make Ms. Manager say, "Oooh, she totally gets this company and understands what I need!" I know you're great. Make sure she does too.

Oh, and when in doubt, go formal. I'm thinking about having my kids call me Ms. Mommy now as a sign of respect. It really rolls off the tongue.

If you're applying for a job, ideally the next stage after the resume and cover letter is the interview. This stage is all about "Tell me a story." Your parenting expertise is going to give you a serious leg up in this part of the job search process because how many stories have you read? 1.5 million? You know what makes a good story and what makes you sit there and think, "But, what happened to the second bunny? Why did they even introduce that second bunny if they weren't going to develop the character and close out the plot holes?"

Perhaps I'm projecting a bit, but you know what I mean. Some of your kids' books ramble for days without saying anything, and some give you a clear beginning, middle, and end with a Situation, an Obstacle, an Action, and a Result. That's the way to look at telling stories in an interview too, using the SOAR method. Whether you are interviewing for a job or having a call with a new potential client, you'll often be asked for examples of your past work. It might sound something like "Tell me about a time that you..." To answer effectively, you need to set the scene, describe the problem, tell what you did to solve the problem, and then describe the solution.

To show you how this works, let's pretend I'm interviewing for the role of Master Potty Trainer and in my interview, I was asked to give an example about how I've managed potty emergencies in the past. I have a good story for that one!

S - Situation

When our kids were born 15 months apart, Glen and I knew that there would be a couple of years during which any attempt to do things would be complicated. Between bottles, and diaper changes, and potty training, if we were going to leave the house it was going to be an event and we were going to be pack mules. We still went places and did things, but on a pretty strict time table and while carrying a diaper bag so large it warranted its own zip code.

Then all of a sudden Norah was drinking milk from a cup and didn't require numerous bibs. Soon after, Jack mastered bathroom skills and we only had one kid in diapers which minimized the diaper blow-out risk. To go out as a family now we could just grab an oversized grocery bag, or a canvas purse if I was feeling classy, and fill it to the brim with snacks. Things were getting simpler, but then we got cocky and thought we should bring the kids to a minor league baseball game.

O - Obstacle

We got to the ballpark without incident. The kids' eyes got all big and "oh my goodness we are having an Americana moment" cute when they saw the field for the first time and they were delighted by the $20 hotdogs they each took three bites of. We then settled into our seats on the third baseline, a third baseline that unfortunately did not have a protective net. I spent the next hour nervously praying that 1) these minor league players were professional hit-the-ball-straighters and 2) I would naturally be a good enough parent to disregard my own safety if a line drive foul ball came flying at our heads.

That wasn't the real obstacle though. The real obstacle came after we decided that three innings of a ball game was about right for a three-year-old and a two-year-old with approaching bedtimes. We got all the way to the car when Jack turned to me and said the five words any parent with a toddler dreads when they are in the no man's land between their previous destination and future destination. "I have to go potty." Actually six words. "I have to go potty. NOW."

A - Action

I had to take action immediately on this one. I did a quick scan and there were no bathrooms to be seen in this parking garage. I had to get my three-year-old to a bathroom stat and the only bathroom I was familiar with was back in the ballpark. If I haven't mentioned this before, college scouts were already after Jack at this point in his life, that is how tall and strong my son is. It's great for potential athletic scholarships, but incredibly challenging for carrying in emergency situations.

Knowing our time was limited, I scooped up Jack, who by the way was donning full Spiderman face paint, and started sprinting down the parking garage stairs while humming "Chariots of Fire." We banged a quick right out of the garage towards the back entrance of the park. I'm sure our game tickets were somewhere in my gigantic purse but there was no time for that. I had to convince the ticket taker that we needed immediate entrance. It was a rather straight-forward negotiation. "Spiderman has gotta go, do the right thing, man."

Onto the next challenge, sprinting up the stairs carrying my dear Spider child while feeling the burn from my thighs down deep into my soul. We made it to the top of the stairs and now had to quickly locate restroom signs and then run the gauntlet of families buying cotton candy, some guy dressed up as a toothbrush mascot, toddling toddlers, and hawkers selling ice-cold beer. Summoning the strength of ten moms plus two, I kept Jack securely on my hip and weaved our way through the crowd with catlike speed and dexterity.

R - Result

We ducked, dived, and dodged and made it into the bathroom with mere seconds to spare. It was a rousing success made possible by my speed, strength, focus, and quick problem-solving skills, as well as my son's ability to hold it. Jack was happy for biological reasons. I was happy because my gigantic purse did not contain a change of clothes for anyone in my family. The ballpark and parking garage employees were happy and they didn't even know that they had the very real possibility of being quite unhappy. Everyone won that day.

In a real interview, you're going to want to spend less time setting the scene in the situation phase, and less time adding unnecessary details in the obstacle phase, but what I did well here was show the action I took to overcome the obstacle. The skillsets I wanted to highlight (strength, problem-solving, and determination) were brought to the forefront by using a story instead of simply listing my strengths. Then the result phase is critical. What happened because of the action I took? How did I improve the situation, overcome the obstacle, take action, and make something good happen? Nail that part of your interview and the interviewer is going to say "Wow, I get it! I want her to come do that for our company too!"

Was that a super weird way to teach interviewing tips? Yes. But it was also a pretty fun way to show how the SOAR method helps you to answer a "give me an example" style interview question. And most importantly, I bet you'll remember it. Storytelling for the win!

CHAPTER 19 NOTES

Interview Prep

In your interviews, when asked to "tell me about a time when..." remember to SOAR with your answers.

S - situation
O - obstacle
A - action
R - result

Try outlining a sample story below with one of your career achievements.

Situation

Obstacle

Action

Result

CUT IT OUT

*a*s my children simultaneously entered the toddler and preschool ages and stages there were certain phrases I found myself saying over, and over, and over. "No more snacks." "Go back to bed." "Please use your manners." "Don't use that curtain rod as a sword." "Cut it out!" There was double the cuteness in our house, and there was also double the chaos.

One of the major benefits of having two kids very close in age with similar antics and needs, however, is that they are great friends. They miss each other during the day when they are in separate classrooms, they have the cutest conversations, and their hugs are epic. Jack will also never let anyone mess with his sister and vice versa. It's adorable, and terrifying.

The most terrifying and hilarious instance of sibling overprotection came in the fall of 2017 when Norah had gotten bit at daycare. I felt all the mom guilt when it happened—"OMG my baby got bit because I left her all ALONE" — but on a practical level I knew that one-year-old kids don't have a fully developed vocabulary to verbalize their feelings and they are also still trying to push bone through their tiny sensitive gums so biting is normal. I also realized that even when she wasn't at daycare we were around other toddlers so the bite heard 'round the world could have just as easily happened while she was with me at a playground, at the library, or at our weekly Mike Tyson Baby Boxing class... Some things can't be avoided. Big brother Jack was not so understanding though. He must have heard me and Glen talking about Norah's bite mark because the next day things got super real at daycare drop-off.

The Scene: 7:30 AM, six tiny one-year-olds were sitting around a table eating cereal with their teacher. Jack marched into the classroom with Norah and went up to her teacher. "Who bit Norah?"

"Oh, Jack I can't tell you that," said the teacher. "But she's okay now. See, she's happy!"

Jack turned to all the little children around the table and his glare turned icy. "Who bit my sister?" He was met with stunned silence. "Who bit her??" he repeated with a hint of rage.

Then if memory serves, Jack rolled up his sleeves, cracked his knuckles, and a lackey showed up out of nowhere to light Jack's cigar. Perhaps he hadn't made himself perfectly clear. "WHO BIT NORAH?!?!?"

One-year-olds don't have a great gauge on when they are being threatened by the toddler mafia so they all just stared back at him for a minute and then went back to their Kix. I somehow convinced Jack it was going to be okay and that Norah could fight her own battles. If I had been the one who had bit Norah, though...man, I would have been shaking in my Velcro sneakers.

I know when the time comes, Norah will stand up for

Jack too. She's not a pushover. Yet as much as these two will protect each other fiercely, they also turn my house into a WWE ring on the regular. Wrestling is one of their favorite activities and the one that gives me the greatest risk of heart failure. Parenting these two always leaves me in a state of knowing I'm three seconds away from wishing I had made them stop doing that sort of dangerous thing two seconds ago. Flying off couches, slamming into the floor, taking each other out by the ankles. Guys, cut it out!!!

Then they proceed to laugh and move on with their days, maybe finding some quiet safe activity to do for a few minutes to lull me into a false sense of security. This usually works, because then I'll go back to the dishes only to hear a monumental crash down the hallway and, "I didn't mean to. She's fine. She's fine. Those are fake tears."

Cut it out. Stop. Give it a rest. All of these phrases we utter in attempts to keep the peace have the same meaning when we're talking to our kids. What it comes down to is we want them to quit doing what they are doing and make a different choice. I tend to prefer "Cut it out" because it brings back some serious *Full House* 90s vibes and in my head, I always accompany "Cut it out" with the Uncle Joey hand motions. TGIF forever.

———

"Cut it out" is an important phrase for us as adults too as we try to make career changes, especially if the specific actions we're taking to try to make those changes aren't moving the needle.

Years ago, I was trying to make a change in my career path within higher education from marketing into a more student-service focused role. Anytime a position opened up that was somewhat more related to student services, I scrambled to put together a cover letter and pressed submit. Some of those jobs sounded cool, but I had spent absolutely zero time researching them any further than looking at the job description. I also hadn't spent any discernable amount of time reflecting on what I actually wanted in a work environment besides a vague directional change. I was just firing away, not that unlike a toddler wrestling with my brother and not thinking through the consequences of my actions.

Eventually, I figured out that my strategy was all wrong, but it took a while and a lot of hearing "no". You get to skip past my years of mistakes by taking this advice though: If you want to stop being rejected from jobs, you need to stop applying. I'm quite serious. Cut it out, right now.

To be clear, I'm not telling you to give up. That would make me a pretty terrible coach, perhaps a worse mom. I'm not big on "give up," but "try harder" is kind of an empty suggestion without giving any further direction. Trying harder can leave you spinning your wheels in a big mud pit. What I mean by saying you should pump the job application brakes is that you need to cut it out so that you can focus, and I mean really focus, on finding and getting the job you want.

Here's a little non-job search related story to help drive this one home. In January 2019, I took an introduction to digital photography class. Years earlier, Glen and I had picked up a fancy camera and while I had used it for at-home photoshoots of my children, I really didn't know what I was doing. There were far too many buttons.

One of the first things our instructor told us right after "that right there is the lens cap," was that if we wanted to be better photographers then we had to stop taking crappy pictures. My instinct was to get all snarky about this, "That's why I'm here, Margo..." However, what she meant was that nonprofessional photographers have a tendency to over-shoot and it's a waste of time. If you watch a professional photographer work, they take their shots and move on because they know they got it. They understand their light, have adjusted their cameras appropriately, and have chosen the right place to stand. Sure, with people you can't predict their every movement, particularly when photographing children like mine who once clotheslined each other during a photo session, but pros know how to set themselves up for success.

Amateurs, on the other hand, take five million photos and only a handful are any good. (It's me, I'm amateurs.) That's the beauty of the delete button in the digital world, but it's also a downfall. Since the stakes are low (no film, plenty of storage), the amateur keeps hitting the shoot button as little Jimmy runs through the sprinkler without really thinking it through. Then they look back at the pictures and realize little Jimmy's feet are cut off and those shadows are unphotoshoppable. I know my camera is full of indoor pictures with harsh fluorescent lighting and poor composition that will never see a photo album. Don't even get me started on my phone camera roll. This habit of taking crappy pictures has gotten so bad that I currently pay Apple $.99 a month for extra storage on my phone. That extra storage is then used for 39 burst selfies that Norah took and 548 blurry jumping off the couch in pajamas photos that I took.

What I should do if I want to take pictures that I'll do something with is take out my nice camera, learn what aper-ture and shutter speed mean, step into the shade instead of direct sun, and focus my shots to take less of them. By focusing on the task at hand, I'll take better photos and save myself $.99 a month so that I don't get all bent out of shape when my children only eat one bite of a granola bar and then throw it out because it's too granola barish. (Never mind, that will still bother me.)

You know where I'm going with this, right? If you keep getting rejected from jobs, it may very well be that you are taking too many shots, and not enough good ones. There are millions of job postings out there. LinkedIn, Indeed, your college job board, Craigslist, etc. If you take a scatter-shot approach and apply to everything, you're inevitably going to hear a lot of no, or a lot of radio silence. However, if you do the work to set your focus, your chance of success increases. Setting your focus in the job search is a little different than working on your camera settings, but there's still a pretty straightforward instruction manual.

First, set your vision. For example, do you love all of marketing, or do you thrive in brand management? Would you be willing to move anywhere, or is your family firmly settled in Boston? Do you want to manage people, work at an established firm, be part of a startup, travel, work from home? Answer all of these questions before you put fingers to keyboards and start shooting off resumes. Next, circle back to chapter one and do the work to figure out what you want to be when you grow up. Heed the advice from chapter eleven and make sure you are following your path and not your Cousin George's path or that nice lady next door's path. Reflect on your career and life criteria from chapter three and match up possible opportunities with what you want. Then go after those opportunities with gusto. This way, if and when you hear back from an employer with a positive response, it's going to be for something you're genuinely interested in pursuing.

One of the reasons I need you to cut it out and go

through these steps is because I adore you and I want you to be happy in your work. The other reason is that I value your time! As any maxed-out parent knows, there are only 24 hours in a day and even if you've mastered the juggle, you cannot manufacture more hours. When you are working two jobs, raising kids, and feeling like you desperately need to make a change or you're going to lose your marbles, you need to utilize every spare moment. Refocusing your job search on positions that you actually want and narrowing down your list of applications is going to maximize your resources.

You won't write cover letters for jobs that would make you more unhappy if you take into consideration the three-hour commute. You won't apply for a job that is exactly like your current role in every way when you know deep down it's not just your boss that's bothering you, it's the day-to-day work. When you narrow your focus you save yourself time by avoiding application writing, interview shirt ironing, interviewing, and post-interview thanking! That time adds up fast.

With all that time savings you could do much more valuable job search activities that will move you closer to your goals like spiffing up your LinkedIn profile and then searching LinkedIn for connections at companies you are interested in. With the names of people at companies that sound appealing to you, instead of randomly applying to three jobs you can send three emails that ask for 20 minutes of someone's time for an informational conversation about their company, career progression, or industry. People love talking about themselves, remember? Let them, then take in their advice, ask good questions, build a relationship and then watch things start happening

I'm not only a peddler of this advice, but I'm also a satisfied customer. Remember that unsuccessful job search of mine I mentioned earlier? Eventually, I landed my career services job at Harvard Business School as a result of two informational conversations I had before an open job was even posted. I took a break from applying to jobs and sought out introductions from my existing professional network, and those folks came through big time! The focused approach paid off in my writing career as well. I was sending scattershot submissions and hearing lots of no, until I paused to find out what content works for various sites, connected with other writers I admired, and built my network in the publishing industry.

This process of being hyper-focused may sound time-consuming and you might be shaking your head thinking that I have given you zero time back in your day with these strategies. However, I've done the rudimentary math on this, and it will save you time. A cover letter might take you an hour to write and then end up in a black hole. An email might take you ten minutes to write, and then a 30-minute conversation could give you a ton of information about a new path and land you an interview. See, math! Plus my clients do this every single day and it gets them results in the form of new jobs, interesting new projects, and career fulfillment. Hashtag goals.

Take this a step further and let's say you go with a wide net job application strategy, avoid networking, and end up with a job that meets none of your career criteria. You might end up getting fired because it's clear you hate your job and you aren't any good at it. That will put you back at square one and think of all the time lost. Or let's say you start a business but you don't think through if this is the business you actually want and you don't put in the work to ask others for advice. Time saved upfront, time lost in the long run. Career development is difficult and you are going to need to put the work and the time in, but play the long and more effective game with me here. It's going to take work no matter what, so make sure you're doing the right work.

———

One of my coaching clients, we'll call her Natalie, was facing a big life change and her situation perfectly illustrates the importance of cutting it out. Natalie had been a stay at home mom for six years and wanted to start working outside the home now that her kids were going to be in school. It was overwhelming to think about putting herself out there and potentially getting rejected because of a gap on her resume. Plus she honestly wasn't sure what it was she wanted to do. As a result, Natalie did what a lot of people do, she started looking at job boards and sending off resumes to anything and everything, going full steam ahead to speed up this terrifying process. Doing so created a self-fulfilling prophecy. She wasn't hearing back from job applications and her self-confidence dwindled lower.

When we met I didn't ask her to send me her resume for review or launch into a discussion about networking right away. Instead, we talked about taking this process slow and being patient with her job search, and with herself. Employers take on average six weeks to fill open positions[1], but that number creeps up and up for more senior-level roles. That's just from the employer's perspective too, so for a job seeker in a pool of other candidates looking for the ideal position, the job search and landing process does not happen overnight. Also, relaunching a career can take longer because in this case, Natalie needed to take the steps to figure out what about her previous work she enjoyed, what her signature skills were, what career and life criteria were most important to her at this stage, and what good work would look like to her.

This is all to say that there were a lot of steps Natalie had to take before sending off another resume. These steps were particularly important if she wanted to make sure that she would find fulfillment in her work, which when we dove into it, she absolutely did. Working outside of the home would be a means of income, but it would also mean time spent away from her kids. She wanted the job to be more than a job, she wanted it to mean something to her.

To get there, we started from the beginning since it was a very good place to start. We talked about her life way before having children, we talked about her time in the healthcare field, we talked about what she loved to do with her kids and what activities drove her nuts. Through this process, Natalie revisited Natalie and honored Natalie as a whole person separate from her family and with her family. She realized that the field she had been in previously may not be the right fit for her anymore, and there were other ways she could utilize her transferable skills in the workforce. Natalie also realized that she wasn't going to wave a magic wand and make it happen.

It was only after doing all of this self-reflection and that we were able to reframe her job search and then focus her time on exploring new industries, looking at job boards like The Mom Project that offered flexible work, and broadening her network by reconnecting with old colleagues and friends of friends who worked in different fields. It was a process, and it took time, but it was worth it because she started hearing yes to informational conversation requests which boosted her confidence. Plus she started to discover exciting jobs she didn't even know existed, including the one she is in right now. Natalie cut it out, and then she pushed forward. Uncle Joey would be very proud.

———

"Cut it out" also brings up another important point, that perhaps isn't straight up logistics and job search strategy, but it is critical to this whole growing up business. When it comes to creating our futures, the ones we actually want, we need to stop listening to the voices that tell us we should want something different. It's hard to tune them out, I get that, but when we do, that's when the magic happens. We stop dressing for the job we should want and start dressing for the job we really want, just like kids do.

My little guy, Jack, loves sweatpants. He owns jeans and khakis but he's never going to voluntarily pull those out of his drawer. Sweatpants all day, every day. I can't blame him either, sweatpants are cozy and warm and there is not one thing you can't do in sweatpants in terms of lateral and vertical movement. At five years old, he is making the choice every day to dress for the job he wants. Norah also dresses for the jobs she wants, which sometimes is an astronaut at the playground. This past weekend it was a duck, and so she came into the kitchen wearing a previously rejected Halloween costume complete with a yellow feather boa. To be young again, right?

But maybe we can.

Dressing for the job you want is usually tied to the idea of dressing up, like Melanie Griffith in *Working Girl* rocking the shoulder-padded skirt suit as she climbed the corporate ladder. That was great for Melanie and could be great for you too, but the more honest with myself I was, the more I was on Jack's team. I wanted a job in which I could wear sweatpants...

Wanting to wear sweatpants didn't mean giving up my adult card, just like trading my string bikini for a practical toddler wrangling one-piece swimsuit didn't mean giving up on myself. It simply meant owning the fact that I liked working alone where no one could see my pants, I didn't like packing my work bag with high heels, and I wanted something different from my career than rows of black dress pants. It also meant shushing the voices in my head that told me that was wrong and I was letting down women around the world by leaving my job; I had to tell myself to cut it out.

When I chose the one-piece swimsuit it was because one of the jobs I wanted was to be a fun mom who created memories with her kids instead of stuffing something back into my swimsuit or standing on the shore with one pointed toe and hip pop to make that bikini work for the imaginary paparazzi. When I put in my notice at work to go out on my own and donated the dress pants, it was because the other job I wanted could be done right here in the home I love.

On the flip side, one of my coaching clients we'll call Abby, found herself coming to the complete opposite realization. She had been working from home for four years managing her own small business and had some success. She was "living the dream" in comfy clothes as her own boss, but it just wasn't her dream anymore. Abby found herself staring at a closet full of business attire acquired during her MBA internships and wanting to step back into those heels and back into a team. She was also interested in mission-driven work, and the stability of a full-time position was appealing, however, we shouldn't discount how important those heels were either. The heels made her comfortable and confident. They made her feel like herself! Once

Abby came to this realization it was time to get to work with the logistical stuff to move her job search forward and leave her couch behind.

Wanting the heels was just as hard of a realization to come to for Abby as wanting the sweatpants was for me. We focus a lot of our energy on figuring out what we are good at, and less energy on embracing what we like. We listen to voices that tell us what we should want and we worry that what we actually want will seem unprofessional or silly or horribly boring to other people at a cocktail party. Focusing on what we are good at is easier and less scary because when you are good at something, you get accolades for it and it's smooth sailing. That is until you wake up one day and realize that you're unhappy and no amount of gold stars is going to fix that.

I can't tell you if you should be in heels or sweatpants. Nor can I say whether you should rock an itsy bitsy teeny weeny yellow polka dot bikini or a full-on wet suit next summer. This is up to you. Whatever you choose, my hope is that you can tell your brain to "cut it out" on all the "should want" talk and fully allow yourself to embrace the idea behind the suit you want to wear. No one else is wearing that suit except you, so make sure it fits.

CHAPTER 20 NOTES

Remember who you are! (Said in the Mufasa voice from Lion King...clearly.)

Write down your goal again. That's where you need to focus your efforts.

EPILOGUE: YOU CAN DO ANYTHING
YOU SET YOUR MIND TO

*J*ack called for me to come into his room one night because he had a bad dream and was having a tough time falling back asleep. I sat on the edge of his bed and rubbed his back to help him settle back in. Suddenly his little head popped back up and he said "Mommy, this is a very special job you're doing."

I started gushing. This IS a very special job I'm doing. Sure, I would like to be having a little me-time right now, but being there for my kids, being a great mom, that is such a special job! I'm so glad Jack recognizes that.

Before I had a chance to say anything though Jack piped back in. "While you're sitting there your head is blocking the light coming from the door, that will make it easier for me to fall asleep. Good job."

Basically I was just a gigantic, but very special, blackout curtain. Cool.

Mommy sure is a special job though, and it is my favorite job title. I've had and loved many jobs, and I know there will be more in the future, but this is the only one that I've always wanted and never let go of. It's the job title that brings me the most joy and the biggest challenges. Every single day motherhood offers me a new lesson, and even if that lesson is "how to get Sharpie off my car dashboard," I'm still grateful to be learning. With every snuggle, every hand held while crossing the street, and every running hug my heart expands in my chest. This is what I was meant to be doing, to be their mother.

At the same time, I've honored the other part of myself that wants something different. Not more. Different. There's the curious learner, the woman who likes to make things, the brainstormer, the teacher, and the helper. I enjoy deep conversation and impeccable comedic timing. Without an opportunity to be witty in a day, I go bananas. There's an outlet that I need to make me feel whole.

When I tried to explain this to Norah one day and inspire her big dreams for her future, she was worried at first. She asked me "Mommy, what do you want to be when you grow up?" I replied that when I grow up next I want to be an author, a career coach, and a business owner. She got a little sad and said "But I'll miss you so much if you aren't my mom." In response, I quickly amended my answer. "Honey, when I grow up next I want to be a writer and a career coach and run my business, but I will always want to be your mommy. That's never going to change. Mommies can keep growing up, and they can keep being Mommy and something else if they want. They can do both!" Norah liked that updated answer, and she even turned the line "Mommies can be both when they grow up next" into a very catchy song later that night at bedtime. Maybe she'll be a mom and a singer-songwriter someday.

In writing this book, my goal was to help you think about what you want to be as you keep growing up and to help you set out down a path to success, whatever that path looks like to you. And let me be quite clear, if motherhood is your outlet and your path, the thing about you that makes you feel whole, then you have found it. You are shaping future generations and living out your dream and I'm so happy for you! If, however, you felt the itch like I did and still do, and you feel like you need something different in addition to motherhood, please don't be ashamed of that. Embrace it. Own the process of figuring out what makes you tick.

Focusing on yourself and your needs doesn't make you love your kids any less, not an ounce. Instead, knowing that you have that feeling and taking action to address it can be a great benefit for your children. You are showing your kids that this growing up business is a lifelong adventure full of steps forward, backward, and sideways. You can keep creating your life and building a career that not only fits in as part of your life, but is a fulfilling and meaningful part of your life.

So, please, go ahead and ask yourself the question loud and proud, what do I want to be when I grow up? And keep asking it over and over again. Because mama, you can do anything you set your mind to. Sure there are logistical hurdles to jump over, but look around you at the hurdles people jump over every single day. Look at the hurdles YOU'VE jumped over every day. You're a juggler, a budgeter, a chauffeur, a make-it-to-daycare-on-time-for-pickup Indy car driver. As a mom you have managed sticky situations, literally and figuratively, every single day since that little human you brought into the world or into your life showed up. You did that. You can do this.

––––––

Before we go I'm going to drag this out a little longer because I'm terrible at saying goodbye and I've grown very attached to you over the past 200+ pages. I feel like we've bonded, you know? With that, I want to thank you and congratulate you for doing a very special job, a couple of special jobs actually. You've done great work moving the needle on your own career development and investing in yourself. That takes work and time and I know you're tired, so seriously, you're amazing.

As for that second special job? Well, by reading my words you have helped me be what I want to be when I grow up. Thank you so much, from the depths of my heart. In writing these pages I've dug deep into the process of embracing who I am and creating who I will be next. I've struggled with some chapters, deleted others entirely, and found myself in a state of flow I have never experienced. Writing this was magic. Becoming who I wanted to be when I grow up has been magic. I'm not crying...you're crying... Except no, I'm crying.

As you continue to reflect on your life and work towards your goals, I hope you'll circle back to what we talked about here and highlight that one piece of advice that really stuck with it. Whether it was a way to jumpstart your career, re-enter the workforce, consider starting your own business, slow down, speed up, or be "crying on the podium level" brave for something you really want. I also hope you dog eared the page that made you laugh a lot and made you feel less alone in this wild and crazy ride of motherhood. If it were me, I would bookmark the first couple of pages of chapter five. That's my favorite.

I'll stop stalling on this goodbye and leave you with this. Whatever you want to be when you grow up, I'm in your corner. And if what you want to be when you grow up changes, I'm still in your corner. And if you are exactly who and what you wanted to be when you grew up right now, I'm cheering for you super loudly from your corner.

I'm not alone in any of those corners either. Look around at all the people in your life that will proudly be in your corner, today, tomorrow, and always. Your friends, your colleagues, your spouse, your family, and real specifically I'm talking about those tiny humans you are raising. The ones that made you Mommy. See how they look at you, like you hung the moon and the stars, like you have the answers, like you can do ANYTHING.

Guess what?

They're absolutely right. You can.

So Mommy, what do you want to be when you grow up?

NOTES

1. What Do You Want To Be When You Grow Up?

1. Timothy Butler, *Getting Unstuck: How Dead Ends Become New Paths* (United States: Harvard Business Press, 2007)

2. You Need to Share

1. Jennifer Fulweiler, *One Beautiful Dream: The Rollicking Tale of Family Chaos, Personal Passions, and Saying Yes to Them Both* (United States: Zondervan, 2019)

5. Use Your Imagination

1. "U.S. Consumers Are Shifting the Time They Spend with Media." Nielsen, 19. Mar. 2019, www.nielsen.com/us/en/insights/article/2019/us-consumers-are-shifting-the-time-they-spend-with-media
2. Manoush Zomorodi, *Bored and Brilliant: How Spacing Out Can Unlock Your Most Productive and Creative Self* (United States: St. Martin's Press, 2017)
3. Shonda Rhimes, *Year of Yes: How to Dance It Out, Stand In the Sun and Be Your Own Person.* (United Kingdom: Simon & Schuster, 2015)

6. Use Your Words

1. Spice Girls, "Wannabe." *Spice*. Virgin Records, 1996.

7. Make New Friends

1. Francesca Gino, *Rebel Talent: Why It Pays to Break the Rules at Work and in Life.* (United States: Dey Street Books, 2018)

8. Follow the Rules

1. Craig Ballantyne, *The Perfect Day Formula: How to Own the Day And Control Your Life* (Canada: Craig Ballantyne, 2015)

9. Life's Not Fair

1. Ijeoma Oluo, *So You Want to Talk About Race?* (United States: Basic Books, 2018)

10. Own Your Choices

1. Jim Clifton, "The World's Broken Workplace." *Gallup.com,* Gallup, 13. Jan. 2020, https://news.gallup.com/opinion/chairman/212045/world-broken-workplace.aspx

13. I'll Check On You

1. Gretchen Rubin, *Four Tendencies: The Indispensable Personality Profiles That Reveal How to Make Your Life Better (and Other People's Lives Better, Too).* (United States: Potter/Ten Speed/Harmony/Rodale, 2017)
2. Lindsay Schlegel, *Don't Forget To Say Thank You: And Other Parenting Lessons that Brought Me Closer to God,* (United States: Ave Maria Press, 2018)

15. Believe in Yourself

1. Ben Rector, "Fear." *Brand New.* Aptly Named Recordings, 2015
2. Hal Elrod, *The Miracle Morning: The Not-So-Obvious Secret Guaranteed to Transform Your Life (Before 8AM).* (United States: Hal Elrod International, 2012)
3. Catherine Moore, "Positive Daily Affirmations: Is There Science Behind It?" PositivePsychology.com, 16 Mar. 2021, positivepsychology.com/daily-affirmations/
4. Amy Cuddy, "Your Body Language May Shape Who You Are." TED, June 2012, www.ted.com/talks/amy_cuddy_your_body_language_may_shape_who_you_are

17. Money Doesn't Grow On Trees

1. Kayla Fontenot, et al. "Income and Poverty in the United States: 2017." The United States Census Bureau, 16 Apr. 2019, www.census.gov/library/publications/2018/demo/p60-263.html.
2. Courtney Connley, "More than 860,000 Women Dropped out of the Labor Force in September, According to New Report." CNBC, 2 Oct. 2020, www.cnbc.com/2020/10/02/865000-women-dropped-out-of-the-labor-force-in-september-2020.html.

18. No One Goes to the Circus to See a One Ball Juggler

1. Elizabeth Gilbert, *Big Magic: Creative Living Beyond Fear.* (United States: Penguin Publishing Group, 2016)
2. Laura Vanderkam, *168 Hours: You Have More Time Than You Think.* (United States: Penguin Books, 2010)

20. Cut It Out

1. Martha White, "Here's How Long It Really Takes to Get a Job." Money, 20 Oct. 2015, money.com/money/4053899/how-long-it-takes-to-get-hired/.

ACKNOWLEDGMENTS

Writing *When Mommy Grows Up* was a journey that involved many late nights, many early mornings, many handfuls of chocolate chips, and many wonderful people who made this dream a reality.

Thank you to Callie Metler and Clear Fork Media for believing in this book and helping bring it to life. Your partnership and guidance throughout this process has been invaluable. Another big thanks goes out to Lindsay Schlegel, the first pair of editing eyes that went through these pages. You told me what was funny, what was helpful, and what was nonsense (and the early version was a lot of not helpful, not funny nonsense.) You're incredible.

To the Career Coaching team at Harvard Business School who taught me how to be a coach, thank you for encouraging me to combine expert frameworks with my authentic self and style. Your support throughout my career has meant everything. That same thanks goes to all my coaching clients who have trusted me and made me so proud. You're doing incredible things out there in the world and I'm thrilled for you.

Thank you to the Horan, Atkinson, Carnahan, and Stevens families who have cheered me on every step of the way. You've helped me figure out what means the most and then chart this path forward into a life and career I love. I love you all. Thank you also to my friends who keep me laughing when times are hard, pick me up when I fall down, and help me move forward with encouragement and sage advice. Childhood friends, college friends, parenthood friends, and writing friends. You're all amazing.

To my parents and brother, thank you for teaching me to laugh at myself, trust myself, and be myself, and for giving me plenty of childhood Becca material to work with. To my husband, Glen, thank you for listening to me read this book aloud 14 thousand times, believing I could do this well before I did, and loving me even when I'm being a pain in the neck stress ball. I love you.

And to my kids, Jack and Norah. The people who made me Mommy. Thank you for being you. Without you, this book would NOT have been funny. Without you, this book wouldn't exist. Without you, I'm not me. I love you to the moon and back.

ABOUT THE AUTHOR

Becca Carnahan is a mom of two, writer, and career coach from Massachusetts. She coaches at Harvard Business School and with her company, Becca Carnahan Career Coaching & Communications. Becca is also the founder of the working mom humor and career blog, With Love, Becca, and the author of Belinda Baloney Changes Her Mind, a children's book that reminds kids and adults that they can have lots of big dreams and change course along the way.